BIG FOOT A BETTY LOU SHERIFF BOTTOM MURDER MYSTERY COMEDY

a ridiculous tale of dark woods and healed friendships, illustrated

Keith Hulse

ISBN:9798844627361
Cover design by: Art Painter
Library of Congress Control Number: 2018675309
Printed in the United States of America

Dedicated to The Alaskan Triangle and Big Foot

CONTENTS

BIG FOOT, A BETTY LOU SPIIRIT GUIDE MURDER MYSTERY COMEDY

A ridiculous tale of dark woods and healed
friendships, illustrated

BY
Keith Hulse
53195

Keith Hulse
Aberdeen
lugbooks@gmail.com
lugbooks.co.uk

[CHAPTER 1] — SHERIFF NATHAN BOTTOM

A Betty Lou Spirit Guide Murder Comedy Mystery or guides if they exist, are never there when needed?

Yes guides, and Guardian Angels, they are never there when you full of alcoholic beverages drive of Sydney Harbor Bridge to waiting Great Whites below, and scream, **"Why did my guide allow this?"** You tell me?

Or walking home late at night rather than spend cash on an expensive taxi, are mugged and your body thrown in a trash can awaiting an arriving dump lorry, oh dear, and scream, **"My guide me here, is it crazy?"** You tell me?

Or walking the dog see a floozy girl needing your attention so let your mangy cross bread off the lead that disappears into the bushes with the girls' pedigree sausage dog to make hot dogs, and the floozy girl sues you for a million dollars, so you holler, **"Where was my Guardian Angel to let this happen?"** You tell me?

Or on vacation in Casino World and all the machines spinning apricots, apples, melons and the sound of coin, plastic, and real coughing out, and you gamble all the wife's savings she took ten years to achieve and LOSE, every penny and wonder why the wife drove away with the car back home, a thousand-mile walk for you, and you ask, **"Where was my guide to let this happen?"** You tell me?

That lets you off the hook as not much free choice apart from, "Should I bet the wife's savings or should I not?" And ogle those waitresses in almost no clothes so get distracted and listen to, **"Bet it all, you only live dangerously once,"** and was not a heavenly guide.

Well, it happened because you were a fink.

Christians would say you listened to demons, me, a fink.

Some believe the bible 'you were born for the job like John the Baptist' who The Jews saw as the reincarnation of a prophet, Isiah and the early Christians believed in reincarnation, **so?** You tell me?

Buddhists think you were reincarnated also as you were last time round in the jungles in Borneo you lost your wife's pots and pans in a rigged card game with traders, why her relatives fed you to the neighborhood python, and was a quick divorce Borneo fashion.

Lastly, there are supposed to be 5 types of spirit guides and me, Betty Lou the story teller is one of them, I think as I am BIG TROUBLE to the living, namely my charge Sheriff Nathan Bottom, and as a girl I know a cute bottom titter and his bottom is cute giggle, and see why I AM BIG TROUBLE, **here we your unseen helpers that crop up in this ridiculous tale of MURDER, MYSTERY, SUSPENSE AND BIG FOOT.**

1...A Guardian Angel for each of us to help us connect to the higher side.
2...Spirit Guides, which is me to guide you away from distractions, for the boys BIG melons, AND FOR THE GIRLS, big cod pieces DECORATED WITH PICTURES OF TED PRINT.
3...Archangels, powerful entities, and bosses of angels.
4...Deceased loved ones, cool and they thought I was dead and dusted.
5   Ancestors that I shamed but they forgive as ancestors.

So, if you are a high elite gem robber, robbing Fort Knox, and cut the electric to the alarms, **think again.**

So, if you are an opportunist thief robbing a drunk sleeping it off on city bench as a pool of pee forms under the drunk, and you run away to spend his wallet in McDonalds thinking no one saw you, **think again.**

So, if you are stuffing a nagging partner into a suitcase thinking you got away with the murder, **think again.**

This is not a religious book **but a SPOOF on Guides, just like that spoof on aeroplanes as they fly about to.**

"Wait till the author comes this side, giggle, we have the rack here, chuckle, the Iron Maiden, laugh, and a patched blow-up doll of Frankenstein, in leopard P.V.C. 'Y' Fronts to encourage repentance, fun," Betty Lou.

You think the After Life was about 'sleeping restfully, someone has to band aid poor Frankenstein when authors use him as a stress dolly, a first step in healing.

"What you prefer to kick the pet cuddly white bunny, of the neighbors daughter, see you in emergency friend."

See, I am Betty Lou, a spirit entity of light, not a demon but a FAILURE as a guide, just ask my charge if Sheriff Nathan Bottom did listen, the small built man who I did like to describe in stronger terms, such as midget with a cute bottom, titter, or dwarf with a cute bottom, or his hat is so big it covers that cute bottom, snigger.

Now I am in trouble as hear an Archangel attracted to my cheek approaching, or is it an angel?

An angel, I am so relieved, I thought I was about to be sacked and sent to the OUTER DARKNESS as a guide failure.

"I am Boss Angel and your guide Betty Lou so, first lesson, no

more talk about 'cute bottoms,' the body is sinful, the flesh evil, guide Sheriff Bottom to wear a longer weather coat so you are not tempted Betty Lou, do this Betty Lou," and I looked at that sheriff cute bottom and whispered into Sheriff Nathan Bottom's head, *"Hey buddy, buy a longer weather over coat, black like the sheriffs of the old west,"* and had a last long look at his cute bottom.

"Betty Lou, did you not hear me, forget your womanish ways, you are a spirit, an entity of The Light, and unfortunately a guide, sigh," Boss Angel shaking a translucent head.

Did not stop me from having a last look at that cute bottom, hey wait a moment, the sheriff has to listen to me, let my words of truth ferment in his small brain and then allow him to think he thought of buying a new black long weather overcoat, and look like a sheriff from the Old West, then trip over the hem and well, see him in emergency or over here, *"chuckle."*

I had plenty of time to peek at that cute bottom, years.

"The Creator made bottoms cute to be looked at, so i am a looking giggle, in the fashion of a brainless pretty ankle giggle."

"WA argh Sad I give up," Boss Angel in Spirit White Noise that is unbelievably loud as entities compete to out chat each other, not to be heard by humans, unless you tune into the white noise on a radio and tape it, and Beholds you might hear me asking, *"Do you have a cute bottom?"*

Sheriff Bottom, his memories

"Well, I am relaxing at my office desk looking out a sparkling window. Just watching townsfolk of Colville River City go hither, and none spoke to another but stayed three meters apart the recommended safe distance for not catching COVID 19, but it was not a germ that stopped them chatting, but a foul murder, for one of them was a murderer, so they thought and accused each other crossing Main Street.

*Main Street, **can you spot** Big Foot, two rattlers, a bra, panties, two drunks, a walker, a sheriff, a cat, a dog, a buzzard, a Bald Eagle, bordello 'Little Joes,' a red bum baboon, two apartment houses, the jail, the police vehicle, an abandoned pick up, a chicken and church, you might need to zoom.*
And those on Main Street talked.

"You did it and where is the twenty dollars you borrowed last spring and we know who murdered her, wink?"

"Rubbish, was your unemployed boys out fishing who bored as only caught goldfish and wanted to fish a woman, and I paid you back in the autumn and is same murderers that I think murdered Cindy Lou, wink."

"Hello all, is Sheriff Nathan Bottom putting up a reward poster or does he need too, wink?"

"That skin flint, is Cindy Lou's mother that put up the fifty-dollar reward for information where her wayward daughter is and we all know where, wink?"

"Was Cindy Lou taking cooking lessons from Deputy Clay Eagle, wink?"

"I heard that and reading lessons from the sheriff too wink."

"And Medium Wendy Lou found out and paid her a year's teacup readings to clear out of town or else, wink."

"Hey, I did not know that about Wendy Lou, what about Wendy Lou?"

"She found out Clay was feeding her cooking to Cindy Lou when they were engaged, wink, by reading coffee dregs."

"I heard was Sheriff Bottom that was engaged to Medium Wendy Lou, wink."

"Well, why did he murder Cindy Lou then fool, wink."

"Maybe she was pregnant, wink."

"With his baby, awesome, I thought that mole stuffed in cowboy boots was incapable, wink."

"No, Clay's baby, why Cindy Lou vanished, wink."

"You mean murdered, wink."

"No, to have a baby out of town, **in SECRET,** wink."

One of those thousand city residential winks made a murderer so why had I not caught the person, because I had no idea who was the murderer, a failure being an old west sheriff in a modern world. Behind me old photos of 'Wild Bill, Buffalo Bill, Wyatt Earp, Pat Garrick, Ringo the Chamelion., well he was a hero in the film, and a lawman.

And apart from those thousand folk there were a hundred children of various ages and twenty elderly people, and that was the population of Colville River City Alaska. Well, the cold dark nights were responsible for the children, and the low elderly people count, *get the snow drift, "a Sheriff Bottom joke chortle and the town was awash with sheriff jokes snicker."*

Think it was my surname, BOTTOM, gurgle, burble, now a deep put on manly laugh from a sheriff who could laugh failure in the face and spit into a spittoon, if one were nearby or did have to swallow, 'oh gawd yuck.'

Anyway:
It could drop to minus nineteen Celsius, as we were in walking distance to the Artic Circle were the cold could drop to minus twenty-two.

Yes Sir, I hear over in Mongolia can be minus forty and in Scotland minus five, we are quite warm when you think of it. "No penguins here," a Bottom joke.

'Yippee yahoo,' as the cowboys south scream when see a long horn stampede coming their way, 'Yippee Yahoo as got five minutes if that to saddle up and vamoose." There was nothing to 'yippee yahoo' about and yes, a stampede was coming.

"A swarm of Alaskan Monarch Butterflies, a million of them, and I would not belive that if i wass you, read on, chuckle."

Loggers, coming to town, a hundred of the thirsty alcoholic burly hairy persons, and there was an inn, on MAIN STREET where folk were hurrying to go home.

"I pulled the fire alarm cord," and shouted into a microphone, "Four minutes," and maybe one of those loggers was the murderer. Not only had our city folk had four minutes to clear Main Street, but the hundred loggers had when they arrived a leisurely half hour before the hundred gold miners came to Main Street, then the fifty river fishermen, then the fifty scientists looking for Big Foot, and another fifty looking for the other monsters living in the Alaskan Triangle.

And ten locals looking for Cindy Lou to claim Mother Cindy lou's fifty dollar reward.

And Johnny Christy the man who never works but is always outside our 'General Store' on a rocking chair playing his mouth organ and banjo. His red hair gelled in a spike that some said he kept his jam doughnuts on, some said he killed Cindy Lou, others said I killed her, others Big Foot kidnapped her and she is cooking beaver steaks Alaskan style for them. This town is full of idiots.

Others that she married a Big Foot.

THESE ARE MY NEIGHBOURS.

They also think I am an idiot as not caught the murderer, yet, are you the murderer?

Anyway:

Johnny a man washed and pressed, and his tartan lumber jacket, dry cleaned looking and must have a wardrobe full of them, as was never out of one, and he was supposed to be homeless by Alaskan standards or you froze to death.

His home, a tent on the far end of Main Street where he had built a wall about it with thrown out furniture.

"There are monsters in The Alaskan Triangle," he would quietly say and then play his mouth organ a solemn tune leaving you standing there like a jerk.

Johnny's trekking brown cowboy boots sparkling from polish and a tin cup at his feet full of donations. Next to the tin cup, silver spurs. Folk were afraid of him, as if he were a civil war ghost or an Alaskan monster not named yet.

Then as he needed his cigar butt to chew switched to banjo playing and soon like the Pied Piper out of a Shrek Puss and Boots Christmas movie, had folks barn dancing along Main Street, trailing gobbler burgers for the town strays to sneak up and pinch, dogs and drunks.
Flashing their ankles,
winking an eye,
blowing kisses,
and all HIS FAULT, Johnny Christy, it was his music, was it enchanted, **that is a secret.**

"A homeless bum,
Disguised drug pusher,
Mouth organ music teacher,
A suspect visiting Wendy Lou,
A murder suspect, sounds better,
The taxman playing a joke on us." Voices from the dark woods, birds, animals, monsters, lovers just happened to sing.

"And we call him Sheriff Nathan **Bottoms**," a non-praising voices from thin air and was a girl-guide.

Now why had I not done what that sheriff in 'Rambo' done,

kicked him out of town?

Well, he was so dazzling clean someone must be washing and pressing his clothes but whom, a woman as we men automatically think 'washer women, woman cooker, bedroom woman, shoe polisher woman, second class citizen.'

Then maybe a man was keeping him? I had no idea and just call me Sheriff Nathan Bottom and unseen bodies did and heard so repeated *"just call him Sheriff Nathan Bottom,"* so hearing them pulled open my desk drawers seeking a hidden cd player, nope, nothing but pencil sharper, acrylic paint tubes and unused condoms that I hoped to use on beauty contestants, women, barmaids, single mothers, the other sex, washer women, woman cookers, bedroom women, shoe polisher women and even visiting female law enforcers.

"Ha ho he ho," was high pitched laughter from an unseen being and unnerved me that they thought my masculine male brutish HE MAN Thor Tarzan thoughts funny.

"Bugger them, I am a lawman of the Last Frontier," and gave fingers.
"Just call him Sheriff Bottom," them voices or was it just one voice and looked about the room for an orb as sheriffs watch paranormal television channels, and this is the Alaskan Triangle.

Then unseen fingers, sure as heck felt like that, gave me a V before poking me eyes, "Oh, s**t did it hurt, F**k you, you unseen loonies.

So, felt my instant cauliflower ears asnd my tongue stretched. But I was a rational lawman and knew I must have done it all to myself, I was needing locked away, but since i did not want locked away, **this is our secret.**

"I really enjoyed myself there, giggle."

Anyway:

Johnny also went to church Sunday and provided a piano accompaniment.

The man was popular, and his name was 'Johnny Christy, cleanest man north of Anchorage,' or should I say, 'cleanest busking musician north of Anchorage?'

And he paid his $25 a month license to busk, well, look it this way, deputy sheriff wage contribution.

"I am Johnny and real name is withheld for secret reasons or The Men in Black visit. I could be F.B.I., C.I.A. Inland revenue, The Alaskan Tourists Board, N.A.S.A. or someone's abandoned child come back to claim an inheritance and encourage murder amongst the inheritors.

So, ask, "What could a shapely wiggly barmaid named Cindy Lou inherit?"

A Colonel MacDonalds Deep Fried Alabama Duck for one, or the big house you all love and live in on Main Street, Colville City, Alaska.

I play the mouth organ as is atmospheric and folk remember prison films where inmates blow into them, to make folks think I am nasty ex-con, and play a banjo to make folks think I am from the alligator wastes of Louisiana.

All for mystery and 'Who is he?' They fearful asked respectfully for the mouth organ chills their souls.

"Who does this Johnny Christy think he is, this is my town

and will drive my patrol vehicle to him and say, "Vamoose or else," the sheriff is in town."

And mouth organ music stopped, and Main Street quietened till the twang of four banjo strings strummed, then silence, then another twang, "That makes five," Sheriff Bottom scratching his chin that was not smooth but covered in 'bum fluff.'

"Twang," another string suddenly, "That makes six, what is Johnny Christy going to do next," and Sheriff Nathan Bottom never drove his patrol vehicle up to Johnny, for he sat in his car wondering what Johnny did do next, so never found out because **it was a secret.**

"Last Train to Yuma," was played on the banjo with mouth organ accompany,ment.

"That boy is jolly good, think will let him live," Sheriff Bottom imagining he was a 'tough bald lawman.'

"Acting a hard type actor but was a squirt, a small man in a cowboy hat that reached his belly button, giggle," Betty Lou who prefers Johnny Christy who keeps his face and eyes hid under a Mexican Sombrero, bet he is handsome giggle, but he keeps **his looks a secret.**

"What the heck?" The sheriff coughing dust from a thousand Hereford milk cows, and the smell of two thousand Texan Long Horns passing pooping as they went, and a Crow Native American War Party screamed by him.

Then all was clean Alaskan air again.

And a banjo strummed, and mouth organ music wafted about.

"Sheriff you alright, you look like you seen a ghost?" Clay Eagle rescuing Nathan.

"Rattle," was heard and both men checked their feet and saw a savage cat run between them, a savage cat that is told about in this ridiculous tale.

"Rattle," and both men retreated to the safety of the jailhouse as no one wanted to stay there, and there opening fizzy drink cans, crisp bags, a pickled onion jar, a sea cucumber pickle imported from China, and Colonel MacDonalds Deep Fried Duck Wings **in a secret bread crumb**, settled down to watch the drive-in movie behind the jailhouse.

'The Mid Sumer Night Dream of Frankenstein in London, England,' was showing.

"Gurgle," fizzy drink drunk.

"Crunch," crisps being eating.

Anyway: More Sheriff memories.

And who was murdered, Cindy Lou, a local barmaid at Little Joes on Main Street. And her photo pinned to a board behind me in my office, a holiday snap of her entering Ms. Colville River Beauty Contest, that brought from hundreds of miles around contestants.

I remembered the unused contraceptives, obviously I was not a Casanova hiding under a moving hat.

I tried not to associate Cindy Lou with that photo as 'what a woman' and here she was in a thermal swimsuit. If she was truly murdered then what a waste, argh, why do I have to think 'men' thoughts, *"because you are a man or did you not know?"* That is me, Betty Lou fed up with the man's complaints and male concepts on women.

"A woman gave us X ray.

Women are teachers.
 Women are astronauts.
 Women are Bay Watch.
Women are admirals and generals.
Men are the bathroom attendants." Those dark wood
singers again.

"Oh, Sheriff Nathan Bottom," heard voice but no bodies seen that
was making me question my mental health.

*

Now Betty Lou must explain this tale for women to cheer,
clap and celebrate with confetti when males like Sheriff Nathan
Bottom get their just deserts and, for men who see women are
for the kitchen, bedroom, and maternity hospital get exactly
that, a career in washing, a pile of cooking books and oven
cleaner, and shoe polish and so are now confident male beings
as they hip hop to radio music oblivious to female resentment, a
resentment that is released by reading this book, and for males
to read this book and see the opposite, male dominance found
in the male Big Foot who are big not only in feet but where men
know is important, opposing thumbs.

Fat chance, anyway I have a job to do, guide Sheriff Nathan
Bottom to a murderer and heaven where he can listen to harp
music, eat grapes, get Thai massages, and jump from cloud to
cloud when bored pinging the grape seeds at struggling sinners
below, **at you.**

*

Nathan Cute Bottom
 Now "time to zero on the person you think would never be
a suspect," that was my other voice butting in, just never knew
to call this voice my guide, a demon, an angel, a passed over
relation, but the voice gave me WISDOM, lowly free advice.

This voice seemed to come from my spirit, so really was
worried but relieved same time as was The Inner Me, my ID

speaking to me, bit of Freud or Jong as can read and do, look, 'Jail Beautiful,' I am beautiful so have confidence to look the world down.

Below Cindy Lou's photo, photos of suspects, two hundred jealous contestants in thermal swimsuits, all colors, dozens cuddling baby bears to look cute, others holding rattle snakes, others Big Foot footprints, a dozen holding baby cougars with muzzled mouths, some beavers by the tail as those beavers have big chiseling teeth and did not like being held up by the tail.
So was muzzled beavers.

Then the Big Foot Find and Keep Television Documentaries, it could have been any of those folk wondering about the Alaskan Triangle where thousands of Big Foot sightings have been seen. Busloads of primate hunters struggling up the mountains searching for Big Foot and never seen again, just another amusing Bottom joke, do I hear canned laughter?

"May the Lord help us from Bottom jokes," and Nathan asked, aggressively, **"What do you want?"**

"Am I dead? Why have you not found me Bottom?" The voice and realized it was female then it stopped, a female and the male aroused.
"You all right Boss?" Clay Eagle entering, I looked at him and shook my head in agreement.

"The voices again," Clay, oh he was so darn smart, "never mind, Mounties always get their man Nathan."

"Mounties, we got State Troopers," I replied miles away with the 'Mounties.'

Anyway:
Why the big wooden totem carved by the local Native

Americans in the town center was Big Foot. Tourists took selfies cuddling that piece of painted grinning wood. Song Sparrows and Varied Thrush songbirds had claimed the head with white markings and in the rare clear days, provided lovely songs.

Then what about the alien hunters, truckloads hiking into the Alaskan Triangle and **never seen again**, a BOTTOM CHUCKLE joke.

And carloads of red baboon trophy seekers as a program said our woods were home to a man-eating red bum baboon, and hauled their howitzers into the *dark woods*, and were **never seen again, a BOTTOM CRACKLE joke.**

And motor and scooters able to ride the dirt roads, as were heavy machines, but the riders with pavilion riders soon walked into the *dark woods* with maps, with X marking a haunted house, for strange orange lights are seen in the Alaskan Triangle, and these folk **were never seen again**, a BOTTOM TEASE joke.

Then the electric cyclists able to ride most dirt paths we locals call roads into *those dark woods* seeking legendary 'wolf shape shifting wolves, and the cyclists were **never seen again**, a BOTTOM COMIC joke.

Then the charted buses with fishermen and paranormal hunters flooding to the Colville River, where reports of a prehistoric dinosaur swam, The Lake Iliamna Monster, and the best salmon fished too, and **were never seen again**, a BOTTOM HILARIOUS joke.

Then folk renting canoes and kayaks to explore our river lake system and picnic on small islands, laughing as they swam and MET the Lake Iliamna Monster, a prehistoric Ichthyosaur, same as Nessie, meet them for they **were never seen again**, a BOTTOM AMUSING joke.

Then monster hunters hoping for fame and glory seeking Tizheruk the man eating horned thingmabob waiting in water for you to fill up your water canteen, then snap, all gone. **And never seen again**, a BOTTOM HYSTERICAL joke.

All suspects, the monsters too, all needing talked to, except the monsters, all fingered printed, not that there was a crime scene, just when the prints put into the national database did come up **'WANTED'**, then myself and my depute, Clay Elk did go in our police patrol vehicle to catch them, siren blaring for the attention of towns folk who did wave and say, "Brave men out to Protect and Serve," then appear in the local Colville River City Times front page as heroes, and I did be reelected sheriff, get to use the car and the back of the jail as a living quarter, with a back window that looked onto a drive in movie park, and better get paid.

"And the townsfolk waved goodbye forever, will not miss you Burkes," Betty Lou cruelly, and my remarks was to teach Sheriff Bottom humility, to hate me, hate womankind, and to never read the bible again.

Who murdered Cindy Lou, I mean was she even dead? Where was her body, another National Park Mysterious Vanishing, where was she, **it was a secret**?

*

"My daughter is missing, those red bottom baboons ate her, what are you doing about it Sheriff Nathan Bottom?" Her mother demanding.

And I produced Wikipedia on the internet with pictures of red bottom baboons and asked, "Any look familiar?"

"Are you serious?" She asked and with that lifted her foot not exceedingly high as the sheriff was a small man who groaned as he leaned against a wall, moaning.

Behind the mother, Clay Elk shook his head and butted in, "Mother, the town is full of strange folk saying even the small people who live in the woods like to steal our children, we are looking at every stone needing turned over, and the sheriff and me even visited the medium Wendy Lou who said your daughter is not dead."

"Is said you are a witch sheriff in the churches coz' you said you see dead people, so have you seen my daughter?" The mother, "and when were you last in church?"

There was no reply as the sheriff edged along the wall away from Mother Cindy Lou.

"I voted for you sheriff," the father saying he might not again unless we found his daughter and forgot there were no sheriff elections in Alaska and should have asked "How we get him Bottom then?"

"Look behind me," and Clay showed them the photos of the suspects, hundreds of them.

There was silence, and I got the feeling the parents were mentally remembering names, addresses and whatever for private lynching's. They did round up kins folk then interrogate suspects both drinking, interrogating by dropping drunk Pikas, Alaskan type of vocal rat, down the suspects 'Y' Fronts, as they pleasantly chatted, then lynched the suspect as the interrogators had not traveled the distance of Main Street for nothing, they had come for excitement, the Saturday night Frill, the ability to shape change into a lynch mob and back to quiet towns folks in day light.

"Well, the town is choked with Friday night revelers, can you get home down Main Street?" Nathan asked to encourage Cindy Lou's parents to leave from the far end of the room, a moving tall fawn sheriff hat with a yellow star on it, the marker where Bottom was, behind his desk as he was a small man.

"I will go with them sheriff as need to question the revelers again about the girl," Clay Elk and I picked up Cindy Lou's folder and followed.

The front door opened, and a rush of celebrity noise hit us and "Mounties always get their man Mother Cindy Lou," Clay.

"We got State Troopers and my Cindy Lou went for a jog in the woods," her mother, these revelers are all too drunk to jog after her and if did catch her we did have found the drunk next to her sleeping it off, it was those red bum baboons," the mother stepping into the Friday night noise.

The sheriff hat was off, resting on the desk, and a handsome boyish face with a long black moustache that trailed to an Adam's Apple threatened to fall away from the bum fluff it was glued to.

"This lucky man was one of those that never grew old, or showed it, he was a vampire giggle," Betty Lou being naughty.

Mother Cindy Lou had a point, a drunk did be found next to Cindy Lou of course, Clay and self, had thought about that, we were law men. Probably why Clay looked at me, his Native American look, he was Athabascan Indian and believed one hundred percent in the red bum baboons and swore he seen them, most of the native Americans living here claimed that also, I never seen a single monkey, not even pink elephants, I was and am a good sheriff and Nathan polished his deputy star.

"Ah, I am going to be ill, hey Fili Pek come help your man, oh Fili

Pek where art thou? And who is File Pek, know any Polish, so, then reader you must patiently wait and find out as what is not revealed is a secret."

Explains why most folks did not venture into the **dark woods** at night in a red cape as those red bum baboons drove you deeper into the woods, then rounded you up, then ate you. Sounds just like 'Little Red Riding Hood,' yeh, we need frightening stories to keep the children out of the **dark woods.**

"Kids you stay away from the **dark woods**," you could tell the kids till hoarse, and the little cuties did run into the **dark woods** as soon as you walked away and "never seen again."

"Sounds like Big Foot," Clay and all looked at alleyways seeing if an ape was dangling in them trash cans eating human pizza leftovers.

"Towns hunted, full of drunks no wonder," the Mother of Cindy Lou, "lacks Godly praying folk."

At this moment in time Clay fidgeted no doubt from an unthinking nervous reaction to Mother Cindy Lou. In the armed forces he did be branded a coward and shot, but here a worse fate awaited him in the physical Mother of Cindy Lou, as Clay tried in one swift action to unlock the Native American Totem to ward of demons from around his neck and stuff it in a deputy striped trouser pocket.

See saw it, he worshipped demons, he deserved burnt at the stake, after he was lynched of course.

He been watching to many 'illusionists on television' so muttered, "S**t," when the totem chain burned his neck flesh as he pulled, then got stuck on a yellow shirt button that pinged onto the elderly beaked nose of Mother Cindy Lou, so his blue chest shirt fluttered open revealing a single chest hair, Clay was Native American, not a hairy European descendant.

Mother Cindy Lou reached out a hand with good hymn piano playing long fingers and plucked the only chest hair Clay was proud of.

"S**t," Clay responded very slowly muffling a "GAWD THAT HURT," and then strangle Mother Cindy Lou.

Mother Cindy Lou held out an arm out the main door and twiddled fingers so the mountain slow breeze took that hair away.

"I called that hair Wendy Lou," Clay rubbing a redness on his chest.

"What do you mean Medium Wendy Lou?" A startled curious sheriff who WAS A PAST FRIEND of Clay's now and perhaps no longer a present friend over, "What do you mean Medium Wendy Lou?" The sheriff persistently.

"I get regular teacup readings in the hope of winning the State Lotto sheriff, MY FRIEND."

And Mother Cindy Lou said it for all of them, "Yeh, if the cow flew over the moon."

"Rattle," a rattlesnake whose sound cleared the jailhouse.

"Spit," Mother Cindy Lou onto a vagrant Ginger Tom, spitting tobacco onto the streets of Main carried an instant $10 fine or the courthouse the next day, with an overnight stay in the jailhouse.

Thing was that the town had no courthouse so and no one

wanted to send the night in jail with her.

"Pay up or Fairbanks and hear the judge there do not like tobacco spitters Mother Cindy Lou," our sheriff.

Clay beamed REVENGE.

"Now I was watching as an interested girl guide and although the sheriff was a few feet off the grounds, he had TRUE GRIT.

And Mother Cindy Lou was so taken aback allowed Sheriff Bottom to get a twenty dollar note, and she got no change, just a shut jail house door on her.

Unfortunately, Clay stood beside her grinning, the last grin he did so for a year or two as Mother Cindy Lou demanded a receipt and change."

"Let me in Nathan Gawd help let me in."

And townsfolk watched as Mother Cindy Lou with her elderly beaked nose unbelt Clay's black PVC belt and pull down his trousers so his 'Willy Warmer ' showed, for Medium Wendy Lou liked a giggle while reading his teacups for lotto numbers that lost.

"Yippy Yah Ho, Three Cheers for Mother Cindy Lou," watching townsfolk who watched repeats of lorry convoy films always making the police fools and the bad guys heroes.

And how Mother Cindy Lou obtained Clay's wallet?

And "A 50 dollar note, how clumsy," dropping it so the slow Mountain air shifted the note sideways.

And "A 20-dollar bill, how clumsy," dropping it so the slow

Mountain air shifted the note sideways.

"Oh, a ten-dollar bill, just what I wanted," then emptied the wallet contents out so the slow Mountain air shifted the note sideways.

And as Clay bending over showed his naked moon but not weenie as that was covered with a Willy Warmer, Mother Cindy Lou, to be coarse pushed that naked bum so Clay fell on his face and Mother Cindy Lou walked over him.

"Free money folks, come and get it," as a distraction for the one hundred thousand townsfolk suddenly rushing upon Clay to steal his money.

"Nathan," Clay called.

"Now the jailhouse door was thick but not soundproof, so where was Sheriff Bottom? Well, I never, there was more than one Fili Pek.
Sheriff Bottom was in his chair, one you could wind up, so he looked larger than LIFE TO LOOK DOWN AT THE GUILTY."

Dear Wendy Lou,
                You better not be doing anything else than reading Clay's teacups, or
Coffee dregs, whatever.
                Your other Willy Warmer Nathan.
        And beside him a picture of a woman in never mind, and
'FROM WENDY LOU,
LOVE to SHERIFF X' on the picture was written across the back in red lipstick, oh yeh, this is interesting and explains why Sheriff Nathan allowed that magnificent specimen of a man outside to Mother Cindy Lou.

"Let us face it, anyone was magnificent when compared to Sheriff Bottom who was just a fawn big ten-gallon cowboy hat on spur boots." A girl-guide who knows she can get away with anything.

"*Rattle*," and I looked and saw in spirit an Indian shaman clothed in rattler shed skins rattling the snakes rattles, and he was a ghost, "*Hey you fink, weirdo in snake skins, who are you?*" *Told you I could get away with anything as I am such a pretty ankle, and knee and bum and censored, snigger.*

And ignored the angelic laughter and should have taken that as a warning.

*

"*I am mentioning myself here as the sheriff is not going to introduce me. I am Joseph, the man's spirit guide who he claims he listens to, but that is blah? As he listens to himself. There is no one more important in this world than the sheriff so why is he going to listen to a ghost called Joseph?*"

I am a Polish gold miner of the last century who was lynched accused of stealing another's gold claim. That means I am a thief, but I was innocent. "*Yeh, that is what they all say,*" quote that idiot Sheriff Nathan Bottom.

He uses that as an excuse not to sit down on a dry fallen tree trunk, make sure no rattler inside first or skunk, 'be silent and listen to me,' the still voice in his head, not that other voice from that b***h girl-guide that torments him with schizophrenic a VOICE, "a sheriff funny's Bottom joke," I borrow, what joke, just an excuse to be nasty.

Really, I was innocent, that was one way more powerful folk already running a bar ended up in the mining business, by spreading tales amongst drunken customers I stole "'*Bald Pete's'* claim and there is no law about for five hundred miles, what are we going to do about it?*"

Well, there is always a handy lasso ready, strange and a supply of drink on I.O.U.'s, unloaded firearms as drunks fire them off at anything and might hit you, so send them to reach me must walk through the **dark woods** that is red bum baboon land, and the hundred drunkards managed it and that is why, their numbers, not one becoming lost taking a beaver trail into a freezing lake and eaten by the Lake Iliamna Monster, a prehistoric Ichthyosaur, or walking into Big Foot or a reservation village and scalped by an angry sleepers sold illegal moonshine, remember this was a hundred years ago when arrows and stone axes were the fashion, and **anyway**:

I WAS LYNCHED.

"*Where is the picnic basket?*"

"*What, we forgot one?*"

"*Never mind this European gold panner got lots of beans,*
And pickled cabbage,
And dried salmon,
And rubbery long dried sausages,
Smells of garlic, he was a vampire,
Only takes one,
And a man with this much food must be stealing our gold,
Hang him.
We already did.
Oh, then let us party, look he has bottles of VODKA
On bottles and 'gurgle yaw wa, European immigrant settler gold
panner moonshine.

Mumm, good, let us toast what was his name hanging out there?
"*Fili Pek*" *a reply.*
What that mean?
"*One of Little Jose's working girls said he told her*
'*son of Penis.*'
Let us drink to that and eat his refried beans.

**"*They stretched him good,*
So, Fili Pek grew another foot,
And we animals of the dark forest
Could not look,
*For we were beasts,***

Monsters of the **dark woods.**" Those beasts praying for humankind.

"And they called him Fili Pek, son of Penis, have mercy upon the thief Lord," the beasts almost forgetting Fili Pek, how sweet of them.

"Yeh, we gave Fili Pek mercy, we hung him, three cheers for Fili Pek and fried beans, and moonshine called vodka."

An in an instant I Fili Pek had crossed over into a new dimension where the blue sky was fine and clear, and chip monks, ground hogs, and deer ran about me, and sang *"Amazing Grace,"* and knew they were singing about me, lucky Fili Pek, son of Peter.

MORE Fili Pek

And the angels acting for a Higher Power of Light after a hundred years of healing said, *"Come with us Fili Pek,"* I will always remember that no trumpets, spirit folk waving bye, medals given, the spirit animals singing, *"Auld Lang Sang."*

"You will be that man's guide," and looked at this human, raking in trash cans back of a pub.

A human with a friend standing near him with a bag collecting what the man found of interest in the trash cans.

Banana skins, mutton and steak bones gnawed clean and moldy pizza slices, "What are they eating leftovers?" I asked my angelic beings; horrid I was to be the guide to tramps.

"You will finish your healing by being the small one's guide," one of the angelic beings.

I looked at the small one, and if the small one became unstable on the box being used for extra height leverage did fall in the trash can and be gone, no longer needing me, FREEDOM.

"JOSEPH?" It was an angelic warning.

"Is it a man?" I Joseph asked as the figure was slim and if female that would make up for being the tramps guide, I could still remember what a woman looked like after a hundred years of angelic heavenly harp healing music and wondered where my hundred-year-old collection of saucy photos bought from a travelling salesman where?

Of floozy girls photographed in San Francisco in billowing skirts waving to me, oh the memory of a flashed ankle, post cards sold to lonely gold miners, yes I knew what a girls ankle looked like after a hundred years, they were shapely boney bits just above the dainty foot.

"Yes, you need schooling as well, guide him well and advance or?" The angelic light shape.

"This," the other and a portal opened and *a swirl of dark wind and groans, gnashing of teeth* heard from heavenly **dark woods**.

I understood, and felt gratitude I was being given another chance on life's physical plane? If my workload were a woman I would look the other way and not at those pointed thingamabobs that women do not have, have no idea what they could be, seen them on my mother cat with babies, I am a good Fili Pek.

"At learning," the second blob of light feeling a mistake was made started to open that portal to darkness and heard *"gnashing of teeth caused by demonic dentists."*

"Well done, already making progress," the other being and then I was alone with these two 'trash canners' with angelic laughter

in my ears, but I was dead, so how could I hear those happy laughs and better, see that slim figure I was to guide.

"Joseph, look the other way, this slim whatever is not a floozy woman in one of your postcards" I reminded, *"see has no pointed thingmabobs that I have no idea what are anyway as never looked at those floozy post cards, and the floozy girls were all in windblown billowing skirts anyway, I am a good Fili Pek."*

Then the small lean question straightened handing a pub menu to the other man.

"Today's breakfast sounds good sheriff," the man reading what had been given him.

"It is a law woman," I was so unbelieving as burdened with hundred-year-old male ideas about female hood, but there was this big shiny badge and no pointed thingamabobs disappointedly a lawman.

"Sheriff Nathan Bottom," my angelic helper number one sternly, then smiled like a child's soft rubbery bouncy television Teletubby all innocence, "Creator Spirit never made us perfect."

"Bottom?" I queried thinking a sexual joke being played, as they were IMPERFECT angels.
"Anything wrong Filipek?" The minor being of Light, and way said sounded as if my name was translated as Son of Penis instead of Son of Philip.

"A fine name," I replied and cringed as I lied, and it showed as a heavy dark weight on me.

"That is why you have been chosen to be Bottom's guide."
"By the way, you have help, a girl-guide," the main helper.

"A girl?" I asked as like the men of the Bible thought girls are for the bedroom, kitchen, bedroom kitchen repeatedly.

"Children were needed to replace those taken by DEATH, Filipek," and knew it was her calling me *'Son of Penis,'* the *b***h.*

And explains why left to cough away Sulphur and stamp the glowing embers off my feet. I better focus or will fail as a guide and be off to shoveling coal way below where a dentist in a clowns mask awaits.

"I love you girl-guide, girl-guide I love you," I called into the Ether but mumbled, *"b***h."*

"A Girl-Guide, you pervert, everyone lock up their daughters," whatever her name infuriatingly.

"I am Betty Lou Fili Pek," and repeated *"Love you love you,"* but mumbled, *"pr**k."*

Angelic laughter filtered to both.

[CHAPTER 2] —THE OTHER GUIDE

"Tis me, girl-guide" and yes you can guess I am a girl. Not Cindy Lou, and if Sheriff *'Trim Bottom'* a female ghost joke, *'did take his hands from his temples and agree with Deputy Clay Elk, he was not stereophonic but had spirit guides trying to speak to him"* I could help him clean up Colville City of the mess the weekend revelers left behind and free me for I did not know if I was dead or breathing?

Main Street Saturday Morning

"A drunk statue of Big Foot as looked wooden with an empty beer bottle in the big ape mouth, it was snoring, remarkable for a wooden statue, **it was alive.**

A taxidermist mannequin of a red baboon with an empty

XXX bottle in each hand and the stuffed animal WINDED, it **was alive.**

A lanky Tizheruk monster with a horn used as a bra holder and not forgetting the men, 'Y' Fronts, a bottle of moonshine lay beside it leaking fluid and fumes so a passing nasty cat that hated Mother Cindy Lou breathed in and passed out to a land full of tinned fish and no humans to open them, and with a thud came back to Planet Earth and p***ed off went to find Mother Cindy Lou as many tobacco stains covered this her or him cat, who cares was a mangy moggy. **They were both alive.**

"Oh Betty Lou, a cat is a beautiful creature, understand?" And was a stern angelic voice.

And local kids running about in dark Ninja Turtle costumes rummaged the pockets of the sleeping drunks so these kids were **still alive later** in the day spending their loot on chocolate icecream with a mango slice stuck in it, and buying second hand magazines of 'Home Beautiful' from Little Joe at his back door.
"A Little Joe has to make a living, besides I wore gloves ."

And the kids, "They are richer than us, we have no industry, no factories, no offices, no prospects, and have U.F.O.'s and a United Nations Charter to Fleece Drunks, and the drunks are our fathers, and unfortunately **alive.**

A hundred thousand hangover revelers just left where they toppled, well, there was only one bed in the goal and Nathan Bottom used it for an early night when there was a late drive-in movie showing and had thoughts of adopting a mangy revengeful mangy cat and had gone as far to leave a tub of cat food and bowl of water outside the jail house door.

And was all gone in the morning.

And regular feeding produces regular number twos that a p***ed off revengeful cat knew where Mother Cindy Lou lived, it had followed her home many times waiting for an opportunity to attack, snarl, jump, hiss, kangaroo kick, bite then run away as 'scaredy cat run away to live another day,' and was song by Johnny Christy followed by frantic banjo strumming which terrified the cat so ran to the top of Little Joe, an easy thing to do as he was little, and used his head as a spring board to land amongst the pile of sixty unsold 'Home Beautiful Magazines,' that it shredded in a second, then jumped in an open window, belonging to Mother Cindy Lou, who started screaming.

So would you if you had a mangy cat ripping you up good, and as the cat fled out that window with a satisfied smirk, Mother Cindy Lou took aim and spat, tobacco juice and a direct hit.

And so the reason why these two hated each other, a vicious cycle.

This was Colville City, population one thousand, that was reached when the Friday revelers visited or might be closer to a few hundred, a hundred then. Locals busily making Big Foot and Red Bum Baboon wooden figures for tourists and strong moonshine to get the badly made figures sold to unsteady tourists seeing double as that moonshine was 200% proof.

No wonder the kids found it easy to rifle pockets.

"By the way just call me Betty Lou and the sheriff has found a picture of me dated 1920 Colville Beauty Contest, and do I look trim in that seal outfit and sun hat armed with bucket and spade.

And I won the contest so just confirms what I already knew, I am beautiful, where is Fili Pek? "Oh Fili Pek, I won a beauty contest, does that mean I am pretty, more than pretty, how about beautiful?"

Then them wooden statues of Big Foot, Red Baboons and the Tizheruk came to life, and as were still drunk did what humans do the next day, stunk the streets up and the humans saw them and terrified ran into houses banging on doors to get in.

"Twenty dollars friend and you can enter," a local behind the mosquito netted door.
"I spent all my money, let me in."
"Try next door, byeeeeeeeeee."
"I got credit cards, see."

And the door opened enough for a credit card machine to take a payment.

"Please wipe the feet before you come in, headache pills a dollar each, ice coke twenty dollar a can, greasy fried eggs sunny side up thirty dollars, a bucket for illness forty and you clean up or my Cousin Shorty here visits you," and shorty was a six-foot primary school dropout.

But the locals made a living every weekend and were rich not needing a United Nations Charter.

And the drunk monsters cleared off to the **dark woods** to wait till the weekend. A whole week for the cute deer's, elks, moose, and lost trekkers not to be eaten as that moonshine is 200% proof, and a big problem exists in the **dark woods** about Colville City, they are full of alcoholic monsters waiting for the weekend.

Big Foot needing Diazepam so sneaked behind houses and kicked the kitchen door in locking for moonshine instead.

Red bum baboons in one horde running through the swing doors of Little Joes and out again with bottles stacked in bins and carted them into the **dark woods** where "Argrsnarl," was heard for an hour till exhaustion overtook the disappointed alcoholic red bum baboons as those neatly stacked bottles were empties.

And those Big Foot being big folks carried away trash cans

and sat about their camp eating bitten doughnuts and dipping them in almost empty coffee cups, just as they seen green faced folks do in town.

They were ill from acholic poisoning and needed more poisoning to feel better, they were acholic monsters.

Monsters that mugged trekkers, mountaineers, joggers, monster hunters, bird watchers, human bird watchers for moonshine, bottled or tinned and got nothing as these were decent folk out to enjoy the **dark woods** and instead had to endure stale alcoholic breath, and never came back to Alaska and so were listed as missing persons by a pint-sized sheriff and magnificent specimen called Clay.

"**They needed to show** Mother Cindy Lou they were protecting the town.

They needed to show those lynchers they were protecting the town.

They needed to show the monsters they were protecting them from the town.

They needed to show Alaska State Authorities they were protecting the town.

They the State Authorities **needed to know** where Colville City was, it was not on any map.

They the State Authorities heard mouth organ music drifting in an open window as central heating meant they could open windows, they had money, tax money to spend.

"I am tired of hearing the same tunes," the State Governor.

"Sir, he plays same to remind you he exists," a smartly dressed female aide.

"Yeh, well he can take his music to Colville City and tell me where on the map Colville City is and we can tax them for road maintenance, law, and order.

"Sir, they have a sheriff and a deputy on our pay roll."

"Fit, hey' Jimmie he needs a head banging?" As the governor was a Scottish Aberdonian Glasgow cross breed immigrant that came to America as a dish washer and because he was in America, made it to a top job, State Governor.

"Sir, Alaska like Hawaii has no elected sheriffs, this Sheriff Bottom is scamming the glorious State of Alaska, sir," the female aid excited over a head banging as things got boring and hot in this top floor penthouse governor suit come office.

My there was a double bed in black sheets, a huge wall mural of a floozy woman on a red sheeted bed, a bar whose acholic bottles glittered in the sunshine.

And many trophy bear rugs inviting folk to lie in them and be floozy.

Yes , this was an office, see, a telephone on a bare polished table and biro and note pad for the aid to take notes.

A private toilet and shower inside a wall mural of a salmon fisherman in an Alaskan river, in oil, and the artist had painted a tiny hairy figure sneaking up on the fisherman, and in the human hands of this hairy thingamabob, stones to throw.

Also 'Do not disturb' sign on the door handle was ready to be flipped to 'Do not disturb.'

And mouth organ music went towards the Bus Station where a red headed man looked for a bus to Colville City.

And found one as commercial activities get to places taxmen never do.

And folk on the bus crowded to the front of the bus as a strange man played soulful mouth organ music under a large sombrero.

Of course, everyone knew inside that banjo were his colts.

And the passengers laid bets as to what color his eyes were.

And many lost as they got off the bus before Colville city.

"Hey driver, give me my betting cash back."

And the driver being BANK closed the bus doors and drove away and these were not climate friendly buses, but the kind that left black choking exhaust behind to choke the daylights out of the betting person.

And BANKER knew at the end BANKER collected if there was no winner,
And a bus driver chuckled.
Grunted.
Gave a hyena laugh.
Sniggered.
Threw back his head to bellow joy.

So did not see the sharp bend sign and drove off the road.

Perhaps if the folk were not all crammed up front the bus might not have left the road, and an open emergency exit window at the back of the bus flapped.

Mouth organ music filled the road as a sombrero wearing stranger walked towards Colville City and thumbed a lift into COLVILLE CITY and got one in a purple pick up, in the front seat as he had taken off his sombrero as the pickup approached, why, because a woman was driving and she saw his sparkling blue eyes and was captivated.

"Any time you need a teacup reading see me," and looked into his thick Mick Jugger kissing lips, and "need a place to eat see me, laundry done to," and Madam Wendy Lou looked at places a man wears 'Y' Fronts and the stranger did an Elvis Impression as the job had these benefits, and Wendy Lou, well, what do you think happened?

The pickup left the road and drove down a side forest road at 200 m.p.h. missing elks, moose, and red bum baboons in the cars way.

And the man strummed the banjo fast stimulating excitement.

Wendy Lou wet her pants.

Never mind the man had read and memorized his maps and knew another hundred yards, the road ended, became thin air and at the bottom of the slope Colville City, so was not worried.

And Wendy Lou pooped.

And the banjo was frantic as the car sailed amongst the Song Sparrows and landed with a greasy lurching all the way down to Colville city.

"Show me where you live Wendy Lou as I need a place to sleep tonight," and finished the banjo solo.

"*He knows my name, how come, who cares I am taking him home,*" Madam Wendy Lou thought.

And her pick up slowly drove down Main Street as folks

on the sidewalk and road stopped and eyed her, as she was a good-looking woman, then eyed the stranger thinking horrid lynching thoughts.

"Must be a taxman, a lynching tonight we go. "

"Must be a new schoolteacher, I hate school, a lynching tonight we go.

"Must be an updated news writer, we like our privacy, a lynching tonight we go."

"Meow," a p****d off cat wishing it lived in another town it could be proud of and go for midnight singing with cat chums.

And Madam Wendy Lou stopped at the front of her door, then squelched, gave the man with captivating blue eyes the keys to her house and as he walked to her front door, she accidently reversed as the man had a cute bottom a woman likes to look at.

"Grr," the towns stray dog that competed with the mangy cat for food.

Then Madam Wendy Lou got into DRIVE and as the strange man entered her house she trying to get a last look at that triangular back she thought only Deputy Clay Eagle owned, zoomed at a hundred m.p.h. down a side alley to the back of the house and through the back gate.

Her reasoning was the object of her ogling, her prey, was safely inside her house, now she realized she was wet and smelled of pee and pooh, "titter," and ran snatching a neighbor's pink washing sheet a drying on a washing line and vanished into her house and back out again as the strange handsome man was at her fridge.

"My washing machine is in my cellar," Wendy Lou remembered and made a break for it there.

"Rattle," and there was the biggest bl***y rattler on the cellar trap door.

Mouth organ music filled the air and a sombrero span through the air knocking the serpent away, that rattled away back to the **dark woods** a peeved off snake but wiser, to stay out of town.

"You better come in and clean up Wendy Lou, I like watching a pretty back shower," and mouth organ music filled the air, "and pick up my sombrero, please."

"He did not have to say please, what a gentleman," an idiotic woman who ignored the part HE LIKED TO WATCH A PRETTY BACK SHOWERING.

"Titter," Wendy Lou smelling past him in the kitchen door and the strange man waited till she was out of the messy clothes and in the shower before he made his move.

His shadow approached the bathroom that he opened and the shadow fell across the bathroom wet walls.
Alfred Hitchcock. asylum music played from the switched-on kitchen radio.

Wendy Lou remembered the film and got scared and asked herself if she was nuts inviting a stranger into her house and shower while naked, was that a kitchen knife he was holding, he was going to stab her and eat her pancreas.

"I am to young," and never added 'to die,' as the stranger pulled the shower curtain back and squirted shower gel onto her and began to massage.

"This is more like it," Wendy Lou no longer thinking she was a murder victim, but who knows, maybe he would stab her with the plastic gel bottle?

Stranger things have happened, and mouth organ music was not played, wonder why?

*

"*If I had hands, I did cry into them,*" the first angelic being over Betty Lou's attitude. This being is bright comparable to a 100-watt bulb and bright enough for pigeons, doves, a Northern Hawk Owl, Common Raven, Artic Tern, and other birds to gather, unafraid of the Light or each other now in this loving glow.

"*She is new to the game,*" the second angelic being, small and a helper to the first, comparable to a 70-watt bulb and as was near the ground, Willow Ptarmigan, Black-legged Kittiwake, beaver, rat, wolf, Musk Ox, porcupines, cougar, and others knowing a truce existed in the glow of this warm Light.

Betty Lou felt at peace and knew she must give that peace to Sheriff Bottom, and wished he had a name change and laughed at her ghost joke, "*Fili Pek,*" and tittered at that to.

At least she was ahead of Joseph who saw his life flash by and even if he was lynched, he ate well, slept dry, and washed his pink long johns so did not smell in the After life. He looked at Sheriff Nathan Bottom and remembered how he first met him raking a trash can, how first impressions can be misleading.

"*Well done lad,*" it was the minor angelic being.

"*Yeh my first impression was 'FILI PEK' giggle, chortle, snigger, sneer.*"

And the first angelic being sighed looking at me, I was beautiful and could get away with anything, so I thought.

"Fili Pek," pushing it.

*

"We are in Alaska, forget being a modern man, listen you your guides, you are gifted sheriff, all my people know that and why we vote for you. From your hands sprout Norland Apple branches for tree animals to eat, from your feet tree roots, burrows for artic ground squirrel, your heart glows in Spirit Sheriff," I Clay Elk told my friend the sheriff and lied to him as my people never voted for him to be sheriff, my people have State Troopers and Mounties as they always get their man.

"I manage to block the voices I hear, fortunately they are outside of my head, or I did be in an insane asylum," the sheriff answered me, and *"sigh,"* knowing his friend Clay was being charitable, Betty Lou.

"Bl***y War***K, w***h, burn him at a stake, yeh, we have not burned a witch here ever, always a first time," Mother Cindy Lou her voice drifting from church to the jail.

"Hey Sheriff, I want to know why no one votes for you?" Yeh, if I was working with the small man I needed to know everything about Sheriff Bottom, down to the color of his socks and does he know his friend Clay is sharing his Chinese Takeaway with Madam Lou and when he finds out, *"Will he murder Clay,*
Will he sack him,
*Will he drop him off in the **dark woods** never to be seen again,*
Will he wish the hap[y couple everlasting mirth,
Will he close himself in the jail and sulk,
Will he to show he can do better and date Mother Cindy Lou and
Will her husband Father Cindy Lou murder him,
Oh, the excitement and glad now I am his guide." Betty Lou

trembles *"with excitement titter."*

"Where did we get her?" Angel Number One who disturbed allowed to much spirit energy to glow and 'BANG' went his lightbulb and all the cute animals ran away terrified, of him, and the 'bang.'

And the angel did not notice a tremor in the Ether he floated in, something else was disturbed by this angelic behavior, never mind Betty Lou, she was only a human spirit, and everybody above knew they were imperfect, but angels were perfect, apart from those naughty randy Nephilim that dated Earth girls back in the time of Enoch when he authored his books such as 'Book of Giants.'
BLAH.

*

"I miss you, you old fart," and all we could see was the back of a half-dressed male holding a picture of a miner, then he tossed the picture into a corner. Lucky there was a pile of skins it landed on, or shattered glass did explode towards his bare feet.

Obviously, the habitation this man was in was heated as even summer nights are cold in ALASKA, the state below the Arctic Circle where Sant Klaus lives, floozy elves pose for North Pole post cards and elves in orange hold ups and green jackets visit Planet Earth to claim back dated child support from unsuspecting humans.

And that is what you get FOR holidaying in the North Pole.

So, we follow this man's gaze about his room, a tightly stuffed Ginger Tom in boots is in pride of place on a mantel piece above a fake log fire, all the bars on.
Stuffed cat, not living, so be happy.

"Ginger" was written on the cardboard cutout dangling from

the cat's neck, sweet, it was his cat, so he stuffed it with hay when it died, the fiend, and how did he stuff it, do not even think about it.

Orange or was it yellow glass cat eyes followed the man about the house, someone or thing was alive in that cat. *"Had the bas***d stuffed his pet cat in a zip up Halloween cat costume, the cruel fink,"* then I felt it, it was a cat spirit and glowed hate towards this man, wow, this cat spirit should say hello to that moggy that hunts Mother Cindy Lou in Colville City.

And the cat spirit telepathically told me he was the worst cat owner ever.

Why he dressed this poor cat up in pink everything, trousers, shirts, underwear, pink sunglasses, pink litter, pink salmon, lucky expensive cat.
Pink bedding.

The cat tells me it went pink insane, meaning all it saw was pink, pink mice, pink rats, pink milk and never let Ginger out, it might follow the singing of a mangy nasty cat in Colville City and some curious townsfolk follow Ginger back here, and that would be bad, "Outside were graves and ghosts sitting where a grave marker should be, and pointing translucent fingers at him, "He buried us here, forgotten, not even a flower, him, that fink that stuffed Ginger with saw dust as well and cotton wool balls too.

At night, the spirit of the cat waits till the man sleeps then knowing it has fingers and a thumb tries all night to open the front door so sub-Alaskan night temperatures can freeze the b***s off the bad strange man.

What did you die of pussy cat.
"Pink disease, I ran for it but this idiot keeps bear traps intended

for the sheriff of Colville City and his deputy to stand on and get killed and be buried with them out there with no flowers.

Like what happened to me, "snap," and I was gone.

And he stuffed me so no vet did record why and how and where I met those bear traps.

This man is a recluse Betty Lou, which is your name as read your mind," the stuffed cat.

And I was scared for Deputy Clay Eagle with that magnificent figure standing in a bear trap.

"What about the sheriff, you not worried he might stand on a bear trap?" The stuffed cat.

"Oh yeh, him too but he so small the trap did close over his head, titter," and the cat tittered to.

See we are not chatting English but energy that makes up THE WHITE NOISE you can record on a recorder or such recorder that records so must be a recorder all right, RECORDER, slowly for you.

Not recorder children use to blow in to make melodies, or bag pipe chanter but one that records noise, WHITE NOISE, spirit people chatting. Does say in the Gospel of Nicodemus

Anyway:

This man can afford electricity, he has money, what does he do, read on, annoying yes?

"He is bare chested, and Tarzan shaped with oiled muscles and smells of manly perfumes, nice. He has thrown his beaver skin buckskins onto his bunk bed and shows PINK 'Y' FRONTS," mm, *maybe not so nice to me anymore, but wait men were pink jumpers, shirts, trousers, golf shorts, swim wear, diving suits, flippers?*

So, is still nice to me.

Hear me Fili Pek, pink 'Y' fronts."

Who knows, maybe Sheriff Nathan Bottom knows him as is name associating, titter?

Then the man picked up a photo of Cindy Lou and smooched the picture leaving black lipstick stains, then "Bitch, you were a real girl," and twirled the photo towards the pile of skins and the picture of a miner.

Then picked up a candid photo of Johnny Christy and held it to his chest sighing. Yes a candid photo of Johnny taking a leak when no one was peeking, but someone was to be able to snap this picture, this man in pink 'Y' FRONTS.
To tell the truth, it was the photo of a man's back and we only know it as Johnny as his name was written in GOLD LIPSTICK across the photo, blurring.

Wonder if Johnny knew about this, and "Mounties always get their man," drifted through the open shuttered cabin windows, enough for the man inside to become infuriated with rage and shut his blinds so violently they came off the screws above.

"Crack," the sound hitting him.

"Think my nose is broke," he cursed and went to his sink to stop the bleed and added, "Argh," as his nose was as he tried to hold kitchen towels to his busted nose so screamed the house down.

"*Ha, ha,*" the man heard not in his head but on the wind and cursed, "I thought I killed you, so stay dead as the dead cannot hurt you," and to whom was he chatting?

"I am a melody of tune,
 See songbirds learn from me,
 I am a rhythm of energy,

See me and run friend,
I am your haunting," the reply, wow, the energy was female.

I look about his cabin, piles of photographic magazines of Homo Sapiens Males, playing on beaches who can drink their alcoholic iced drinks fastest and lying on beds. I WAS SHOCKED, this fink preferred not me, but Homo Neanderthals dancing together.

The fink was a Son of Fili Pek, I was heartbroken, what a waste, what an athletic body, oh, Betty Lou calm down, his body sweat is not for your licking, he is a Son of Fili Pek.

Then a burst of Light and angels singing way back in the portal but two figures stood in the portal hole, shadowing it.

"Betty Lou, as much as I admire you," and was Boss Angel and knew I had him eating out of my translucent hands as I had nothing to admire except my BODY.

"I am made of tougher energy," Number Two Angel not happy at his boss admiring.

"Betty Lou, sweetheart you are a guide, please behave like one," and then was gone satisfied I was chastised.

"I am watching you," the number two angel and pointed two fingers into his eyes to show he was watching me, "ouch," as he poked his translucent green eyes.

"You got cute eyes buddy."

And he was gone.

Leaving me with narrowed eyes and a Cheshire Cat grin, I was something else, *"Yeh, better do some girl- guiding,"* and with

BIG FOOT, A BETTY LOU SHERIFF BOTTOM MURDER MYSTERY COMEDY

a sad look at the strange man in the cabin, sad as he was a waste to womankind, I went to find Sheriff Bottom and impress upon him what I had discovered.

One of us was a real detective.

*

"Now Fili Pek is here, happy Betty Lou," and happened thus:

Now being curious and prompted by the second angelic being, "Filipek, go investigate for the sheriff, go on, be a good boy, Filipek go."

Yeh, being insulting worked and inched into the astral energy waves and followed the voice trail back, cautiously as knew about demons always impersonating sweet cuddly girls, to get you to cuddle, then pooled into a demon you were holding, cuddling, fondling, even worse, oh SPIRIT CRTEATOR forgive me, I am imperfect."

"Joseph, shut up," it was my second angelic helper again.

But the energy trail had gone cold, fortunately for me. I could see that bi**h Betty Lou's trail but pretended not to, it would lead me to the strange man.

My angel sighed and shook its head and wings.

"Filipek, what are we going to do with you?" That was helping, it was a threat.
And the angelic beings opened a portal and threw me in and I came out next to the man in PINK 'Y' FRONTS and Betty Lou's residual spirit energy drowned me.

"Happy now Fili Pek?"

"Love you love you love."

48

And was a lie.

And heard a melody.

Lo and BEHOLD, light filled my vision and other angels with shining wings blowing trumpets, reed instruments and lyres lined the source tunnel that the melodious strumming came from, then all vanished.

"You were not supposed to see that," and was angel number two.

But a glimpse of a shadowy humanoid at the end of the tunnel, it had pointed thingamabobs so was a woman, see I know what a woman looks like, we gold panners know the difference between a girl and a skunk.

Was she not dead, or between our worlds.
I had to get back and tell who?

"You know Number Two, you pass over as whom you were on the physical, and this one passed over AN IDIOT," and was obvious Boss Angel was annoyed, and was hurt he called me an *"idiot."*

"Meow," I heard a cat?

"Follow the cat to whom you are supposed to tell Fili Pek," Number Two letting the vowels rub together as if speaking with marbles in his mouth to pronounce 'PEK,' as if he was spitting out a garden slug.

So looked and was terrified, appalled, mortified, alarmed, shocked, horrified, stunned, disgusted, curious that the meow was coming from a stuffed example of taxidermy.

I was so drawn to the stuffed animal never noticed two

angels holding their heads pulling hair from, sorry feathers from their heads in dismay over my actions.

Wait a minute they told me to follow the 'meow.'

"Meow," and was a faint meow, you mean there were two 'meows?' I asked turning to look for my angelic teachers and was a mistake.

That was one peeved off stuffed cat as its spirit jumped me.

Shredding me to pieces.

Luckily for me we was both in the Ether and I felt everything as my memories of a shredding passed over with me.

"Jesus Sweet Jesus take this peeved cat off me, please," I begged in prayer.

And things darkened as the strange man's guides, dark imps crowded the cat urging it to shred that bit of me that was missed, or that other part.

"Hi Fili Pek, want a bit of help from a GIRL?" Guess who?

My lips trembled trying to agree but I saw in her mind that B***h was adding, *"if you say with a cherry and lick my trekking boots,"* and showed me pink trekking boots Betty Lou had used visiting a hog farm.

"Meow," and was the stuffed cat, well the spirit of the cat that stopped us both being sent to the Darkness where there gnashing of teeth is heard.

For animal spirits come from the same source as we, but are not polluted by greed, war, murderer, lotto wins and so are purer light and was fed up with the dark imps getting in places closed to dark imps.

The bum, the mouth, the eyes, and ears so went berserk and in a comic book swirl of action and tornado energy stood in front of us two a ghost cat, gleaming.

It looked back at the dark imps clustering the strange man and floated over to them,
And peed on all.
The dark imps cringed as cat pee stinks.
And the strange man shuddered and opened his pink 'Y' fronts and smelt and since he had consciously let off, or made a little deposit went away sniffing the room, and then the stuffed cat.

He stood there glaring at it and then laughed, as knowledge flooded him.

Then threw the stuffed cat out into the wild, where a passing band of wolves did take it, passing the stuffed cat to each other as the weight tired them, and eventually twigging it was not a real cat left it on the road.

Where the owner of 'Little Joe's' bar, bordello and illegal casino stopped his pink up vehicle and threw the stuffed cat into the back of his pickup vehicle.

Little Joe as that was his name was small like the sheriff and thought the stuffed cat did go well on the bar below the trophy of the moose, a beaver and a mouse that had plagued his bar.

And he told all it was a 'Scottish Wild Cat,' that stole babies, ate them, sheep as well, and tore down your washing line, got tangled in your underwear and ran through the village in them, and folks said, "Ho, purple shorts and a red bra, hey wait a moment that is Jock's underwear, oh dear," so the cat deserved being stuffed.

And in the bar floozy owner's dangled their Triumph Push Up Size 46D Bras on the cats stuffed stiff tail, as Little Joes was a bordello as well as a flea pit bar locals loved to drink in, as it was a flea pit bar, that you never saw Mother Cindy Lou in, but did her husband, Father Cindy Lou, who Madam Wendy Lou saw all out the back of her bedroom window as she ate a Madras Curry takeaway with the handsome deputy, Clay Eagle, and told Sheriff Nathan Bottom she shared a meal with her nephew up from Anchorage as Bottom some nights read her stories, from educated well written literature, **the sheriff could read.**

A lot times a week the nephew visited and the nephew was a minor so got to travel the busses of Alaska at odd hours by himself and was lucky he was not abducted by a murderer.

"WAKE UP SHERIIF BOTTOM," I Betty Lou shouted through the Ether to help him, but he just stuck a pencil in his ears and cleared them of wax, the disgusting S**t as it was you who came a visiting and stole his pencils thinking you were smart, yeh, smart as went away with the sheriff's ear wax, big bulbs that melted in your pocket, staining your pants to near the waste exit hole, how embarrassing and for the Sheriff, explains why he was deaf, the unhygienic slob.

And Madam Wendy Lou was two timing them both, what did she tell Clay Eagle when he found books like Moby Dick covered in crisp crumbs, "My nephew visited from Anchorage and the sweet thing believed the two-timing hussy, poor wonderful Clay was heading for a broken heart.
And Madam Wendy Lou from her back window when watching drive in movies free, often saw Father Cindy Lou push open his window and try to jump out silently.

Sometimes he made it when Mothe Cindy Lou did not shout, "Shout the Bl***y window moron, it is freezing, then go cook me a roast elk as I am hungry, and do not forget to stuff it with a beaver stuffed with pumpkin as my vegetable."

Then Father Cindy Lou remembering to wear knee high fishing Wellingtons jumped across the slithering rattlers to Little Joes, and the Chinese Takeaway next door and ordered a roast elk, stuffed with a beaver stuffed with pumpkins, and the other times he did not make it out the window when Mother Cindy Lou hollered he fell the six feet from the window to the ground praying to God there was no rattler underneath him, or he was a goanna, for sure he was.

And by the time the Chinese chef cooked his roast elk stuffed with beaver stuffed with pumpkin, Father Cindy Lou had a wonderful time and caught S.T.D. and thank goodness Mother Cindy Lou was practicing chastity as she was a God-fearing woman, a matron of her church.

And the local doctor made a fortune out of Father Cindy Lou prescribing antibiotics as America does not have a free National Health Service like other countries.

"Use contraception," the doctor would advise but the fool knocked back the moonshine and forgot all about those rubber balloons thingamabobs so deserved what he caught.

And on the way home was smelling of moonshine so sprayed lavender deodorant all over himself to fool his wife.

A wife who was watching him from her back window six feet up from the ground.

And when Father Cindy Lou's fingers gripped the window ledge, a miracle happened, the window shut by itself on ten fingers.

Father Cindy Lou could not scream as he was afraid he did alert his nasty wife who practiced chastity, and with a cheating husband full of S.T.D., no wonder, and maybe if she had invested in discount old Christmas sale saucy bedroom stuff he might not be hanging from a closed window.

"Rattle," he herd underneath him and Father Cindy Lou drunk as he was prayed to everyone's Gawd, "I am sorry I messed up, please help me, there is a ten-foot rattler under me, and 'Jesus Christ' it is so big it is able to reach me, oh Gawd save me," and every one's Gawd did.

A mangy demented savage cat hating him full of red glowing eyes borrowed from hell saw him, and in its eagerness to shred his back took the rattler out.

And the mangy cat was well fed that night, and lucky the rattler was focused on biting Father Cindy Lou or might be a different ending for that mangy mean moggy.

And in the morning Mother Cindy Lou would open the window and stretch, yawn, and say, "Oh what a wonderful morning," and burst into hymn, even though it was soaking outside as rained all night.

And never once looked down.

Perhaps she was hoping for a divorce from the help of pneumonia.

And Father Cindy Lou fell six fee to the ground and if you asked him what he saw from his stretched hanging position, "Big Foot, Red bum baboons, Little People raiding Lille Joes trash cans for moonshine dregs and the Chinese and Indian takeaway for spicy food.

And not fancying that, pizza slices from the pizza takeaway.

So well fed these monsters of The Alaskan triangle they left Father Cindy Lou alone.

And he did catch pneumonia and spent the next two weeks in the cottage hospital and Mother Cindy Lou said, "Will not be one rattler I put underneath you but six next time."

"Oh dear, and was so distracted forgot where I was going, oh yeh, back to the 'Strange Mannie.'

*

And the cat spirit went and purred all over Betty Lou and was so happy it was out of here; it was even happier it was away to live in a bordello as this cat liked girls.

And hissed loudly at me, "hiss," it went the nasty spirit cat. This cat disliked boys.

Then the strange man lit sage sticks and waved them about us, obviously he could see our two white bright orbs for it is said, 'sage gets rid of ghosts and mice in your, house.'

Oh, what a relief, my orb was bright and shiny.

"Shut up Fili Pek and you go tell the Sheriff what you saw, someone is not dead yet, bet you it is the murdered girl Cindy Lou and if I am right, you got to write a hundred times,
"I love Betty Lou,
  I hate Fili Pek," all right."

I never bothered to answer but followed the second 'meow,' and it took me to a mangy moggy outside the sheriff's jailhouse.

There was my human physical, Sheriff Bottom sitting in his

police patrol vehicle with the window down, rather than sit on the jailhouse porch in a chair, then his legs did dangle as they did not be touching solid ground.

"Shrimp," kids did shout then run.

The man was small, I wanted to be Clay Eagle's guide as was tall, strong, handsome, clever, everything I wanted to be as a human physical.

"Ouch," as felt this bolt of energy hitting me, what had I done wrong?

"I know and not telling you Fili Pek and is that Angel Number Two pushing a barrow full of COAL into that portal, remember the one that is dark," and was smart Alec me.

"I really hate that woman guide and got frazzled again."

So, smoldering went inside the mind of Nathan Bottom.
 It was empty.

Not a thought on solving a heinous murder but then I had forgot my experience.
In his hands a Play Station Games Console stuck at level one.
An unwrapped chocolate bar next to him.
A mouth needing wiped of chocolate.
Pictures of women on the patrol vehicle dashboard, the man was a pervert.
"Idiot, those women are the women," and I stopped at that as did not know what women?

"Betty Lou, are you going to help me?"

"Nawa, just screw you up so you look foolish."

"Why Betty Lou, what I ever done to you?"

"You are a man and I am a woman, different see, I am suffragette and you a Male fool, women for President hip, hip hooray." And almost added women for 'GODHEAD,' but stopped myself as saw Boss Angel shaking his head and looked like he was coming my way.

"Suffragette, Sweet Jesus save me."

"When you two are quite finished, have you not a message to deliver one of you," Boss Angel and the way Boss Angel looked at me knew he was a male angel and Fili Pek was doomed.

I tittered and dropped a pocket religious book and bent down to retrieve it.

Boss Angel **knew I could have thought the bible back as all existed in MIND, so did I, but then** I had a chance to scratch my translucent left long shaven adorable woman ghostly leg.
For an instant Boss Angel froze.
Girl legs have that power.

"What you looking at Boss?" Angel Number Two and looked so scratched a bit higher.

Number Two was a Number Two as gaped waiting for more translucent leg to appear.

"Translucent fleas, must have pinged of Fili Pek."

"Garr, woman," and Fili Pek leapt at me, his mental energy knocking me over.

I made sure lots of leg, ankle, knees, elbows, and only little bits of the melons showed, a woman knows how to win, and cried lots of crocodile tears.

And Fili Pek was shook like a wet dog by Boss Angel, after a long time.

A long time.

I had won.

"Fili Pek what is your mission here?" Boss Angel asked.

"Help Sheriff Bottom?"

And mouth organ music drifted on the wind as Johnny Christie approached.

A mangy moggy cat got more excited as had been watching us.

Johnny was good for a scratch and cuddle.

And melodious singing filled the interval to be noticed.

>   **"Chirp tweet went the song gathering birds,**
>   **Oh, the little darlings,**
>   **Out of reach of the moggy cat,**
>   **Whom they whitened,**
>   **As these were Alaskan songbirds,**
>   **No one tried to eat them,**
>   **And never forgot whom,**
>   **So, poor mangy moggy."**   Tweeters and chirpers informing you why the mangy moggy got it.

And *"idiot, tell him about me."* The melodious singing changed to an angry voice.

You know I was so wrapped up being mean to Fili Pek darn well forgot who, what, see and tell all to who?" It was time to scratch the translucent bum and make sure the hem of my smock inched up to bum cheek level.

"Fili Pek, tell Betty Lou please," Boss Angel as Number Two watched my scratching to the last. Then Number Two stuck two fingers in his eyes and then at me, **he was watching me**, that I already knew.

Three cheers for a ghostly female bum.

"Blurb," Fili Pek replied unable to think as BOTTOM and BUMS were stuck in his mind.

"Go back from whence you started and remember or else, FILI PEK," and Fili Pek was gone, just like that.

"You may assist him; poor Fili Pek needs all the help available."

"At once Boss Angel," I knew how to jump to it and was gone.

"Save me," the melodious song and the songbirds took it up in chirp and tweet music, "Save me," the animals of the **dark woods** called, *"Save me,"* the wind blew.

And Father Cindy Lou over his bad cold, was practicing the church organ began to play 'Jump To It,' by Aretha Franklin, so was slapped on the back of head many times by Mother Cindy Lou who whispered, "Do that again Sunshine and I poison your food, who knows ,maybe I already am."

But Johnny Christy played it under his extra-large sombrero that hid his blue twinkling dazzling stare you out blue hard eyes.

And Clay Eagle arrived, "I hear you melodious song; I will save you," Clay shouted into the wind.

"I heard her too," Sheriff at the window of his police patrol vehicle, "let us find her Clay, and be heroes."

"*Save me from this lot oh God save me from this lot,*" the melodious song went.

And a peeved of cat entered a church attracted by the music knowing the parents of Cindy Lou did be there, parents it seemed to loath.

And daintily silently walked quickly along the pews jumping to a new pew, until it climbed to the top of the organ enclave and looked down.

There was Mother Cindy Lou chewing tobacco ready to spit.

There was Father Cindy Lou who on his wife's orders was to broom the mange moggy off the church raised entrance steps. He looked white as a sheet as was thinking 'Is there arsenic in my porridge?"

The mangy moggy took them both out.

Dropped on her so she spat tobacco into her husband's face.

"I am blinded, Oh God I am sorry I took cash out of the collection box; I am sorry I ogled the back of our woman pastor," as hot tobacco juice stung his eyes and after that more was to follow the fool, '*silence is golden.'*

And the mangy moggy ran to live and fight another day via Father Lou's 'crutch.'

"I been neutered woman."

But his wife smarting from claw rakes was in no merciful mood upon hearing his confession.

Using a heavy organ musical book, she beat the hell out of her husband.

And mouth organ music filled the church as Johnny Christy filled the entrance.

The beating stopped.

"Who are you?" Mother Cindy Lou asked.

A sombrero was raised so she saw them blue cold eyes that out stared you.

Mother Cindy Lou was aghast as sunlight flooded in from the stained-glass windows blinding her.

When she opened her eyes again, Johnny was gone.

"I am sorry, please forgive me," Father Cindy Lou of his wife.
"Why was he still here, the perfect opportunity to slither away with the cat and he stays."

She used the collection tray to whack the back of his head.
Only Mother Cindy Lou left the church and at the church entrance steps peered to see where that mysterious handsome stranger Johnny Christy had gone.

Behind her Father Cindy Lou, if he got any more beatings from his wife did either be buried or hospitalized.

All he had to do was leave her, but this was Alaska where marriages were made to last.

And he was watching stars, angels, Boss angel perhaps, as Mother Cindy Lou whacked good.

And just as Mother Cindy Lou saw a Police Patrol Vehicle leave town, she thought she saw Johnny Christy lying across the big back fenders American cars have.

And he put two fingers to his eyes then at her.

"I am watching you," he was saying.

And Mother Cindy Lou was not sure to be infuriated as no one did that to her, but she did tuck down her frontage so FLESH SHOWED, it was Johnny's eyes.

And a mangy moggy saw a running chance to rake the back of her legs.

And did so, so Mother Cindy Lou collapsed trying to hold the railings.

"Look a drunk," a customer at 'Little Joe's.'

Mother Cindy Lou was in a rage, someone close was going to pay for this embarrassment, wonder who?

And that someone came out of church and a lit cigar butt pinged from the back of a car fender, aid by kinetic moving energy, reached him. It landed on his beaver hat and smoldered.

And faint mouth organ music reached him, so did smoke, something was on fire.

*

"I hear the melodious repetitive song Clay, we are going down this lumber jack road Clay at 90 m.p.h. Clay," Sheriff Bottom about to explain to his deputy why they were speeding, and we did like to know why too.

" I hear the melodious repetitive song Nathan; it gets boring after a while and guess we are speeding to a crime scene and explains why we are doing 120 m.p.h. sheriff?"

A worried deputy as smashing into those giant Alaskan Cedars did squash the police patrol vehicle and the occupants to bird seed sized marbles.

And both men saw their life pass by their eyes as the police patrol vehicle was bouncing about, swaying, leaping, bucking, just like a Fairground police patrol vehicle an adult after an adrenalin rush did put a dollar in the slot, and then the amusement police vehicle went into action, and there was sick leading away from the amusement police vehicle.

Gobbler burgers, triple cheeseburgers with and without gherkins, fish burgers, chicken burgers, vegan burgers and empty forty-gallon cans of caramel drink, and a giant queue outside a lonely mobile outhouse, where a town council employee was digging a hole for the mobile outhouse to be shifted over once that hole was full, then filled of course for hygenic reasons.
Alaska has flys to like the rest of the world.

Another town council worker stood ready with an insect spray and shovel to fill in the rapidly filling hole. See, told you the hole was filled.

Already six holes had been dug.

Why, the City of Colville was starting to celebrate the 4th July.

Colville was only a small village, with the Friday Night specials the population went up to a thousand, and Monday back to a miserable hundred.

Why the miserable town councilors were not spending a fortune digging up soil and laying down plumbing, plumbing that went nowhere.

"To the river and our waste can reach Fairbanks, think of the tourist trade it will bring back," an idiot.

"Yes, the water will be poisoned and the mosquitto problem solved," idiot number two.

"Or will good dry it, bag it, sell it as fertiliser," a potential Mall owner.

But everyone had a septic tank and the locals who operated the 'Empty a Septic Tank," were rich, obviously not the potential Mall owner.

And the flying insects were fat and jolly.

Anyway; "I have confessing Clay," Nathan about to lose a friend as thinking he was about to die, wanted to tell Clay he was thinking of marrying Madam Wendy Lou.

"Strange friend Nathan, I have a confession also," as Clay KNEW did not know he was about to visit permanently his 'Happy Hunting Grounds,' when he told Nathan he was wanting to marry Madam Wendy Lou.

And their friendship would end.

Yet fate wanted them not to murder each other as fate wanted to kill them off fate's way so, "We hit the tree and the vehicle is on fire, where was my Guardian Angel, where was my guide, they are supposed to guide me, into a tree so I am burned to death, rich one".

The police patrol vehicle left the road and luckily for the

lawmen zoomed through a gap in the giant Alaskan Pine Trees and: "Oh, Sweet Jesus we are sailing," Sheriff Nathan just before the car dipped down so if he were not wearing a seat belt, he did have smeared the front wind screen in saliva, and added, "Sweet Jesus in your name Gawd forgive me and save me," then "Please" as he could see moving ants way below in Colville City as ants queued for a mobile latrine.

"Oh, Tonka we are abseiling," Deputy Clay Eagle as the police patrol vehicle skimmed from treetop to treetop. "Great Spirit take me home where beaver swim and buffalo roam," and as he saw ants queuing outside the new mobile latrine and the old one getting filled, "we are going to hit them," and held his nose.

"I hope they fill in that hole quick before we land friend," Sheriff Bottom and still friends and not confessed that in the twenty years of friendship had always dated the same Ms. Lou.

Just poor laziness to search Alaska for a single Ms. Lou.

"Ten, nine, eight, seven, six, five, four, Tonka we hit the new mobile latrine and taken it with us, sorry friend gold panner, nice striped shorts you got," as the police patrol car head into the old hole and a soft landing.

"Squelch."

"I have lost my faith Clay," Nathan Bottom dripping what is in a latrine outhouse hole.

"You left the window open Sheriff," Clay wondering why he was Nathan's friend as a strand of pink loo paper weighed down by wetness fell off his deputy hat rim onto his nose, where it slid and plunked in his lap.

"Hey Sheriff, yeh you idiot, I am not voting for you and I

want my trousers back alright," a citizen who was in the mobile latrine.

"Start her up Sheriff and let us escape this crowd forming as looks like a lynch mob," Clay fingering his colt but "squelch," followed by a stink.

"Vroom," the V8 patrol vehicle engine and the wheels span showering the crowd with nightsoil manure but cleared, and left behind a lasso ready for a lynching, for cattle, horse, gold jumpers and manure spreaders.

And the police patrol vehicle sped away and stopped outside Madam Wendy Lou's.

"Madam Wendy washes my clothes when I am in a hurry," Nathan Bottom not adding he would be nude.

"Yeh Sheriff, she washes my smalls when I am in a hurry," Clay describing what Madam Wendy washes.

There was a pregnant silence.

"Well that beat all, Madam Wendy operates a Chinese Laundry service," Sheriff Bottom and laughed, a forced laugh, now full of suspicion why his deputy visited one of his girlfriends, soon to be an unemployed deputy lawman.

"Polishes my leather cowboy boots, shines up my brass buttons, oils my Colt, and just no one else touches my Colt six shooter, and" Clay needed to shut up as murderous thoughts flooded his friend, **"she does not do any of them things for me."**

*

A sweet female sing song voice melody was heard, so even, the six grizzlies stopped frolicking with mamma grizzly, these bears definately not in the 'Goldilocks and the Three Bears Story and **foolish** Godilocks is missing out.

The skunk about to stream poisonous stinky gas into a cougars face hesitated and did the cougar take this heaven-sent opportunity to eat the skunk, no, it been scented before but was entranced by the female human musical script, **this fine zoological specimen of an animal fool.**

Did the beaver plug the hole in the dam it spent most of the year making, no, it dropped the vital chunk of wood and listened to the rhythmic series of musical tones arranged to give a pleasing effect as water pressure built up behind the dam, this **wildlife fool.**

Did the hunter with a good aim on a mysterious muscular hairy beast in the **dark wood** fire and have his trophy and be believed he killed BIG FOOT, and did the mysterious beast run away or charge the hunter, no, both listened to the heavenly solo choir singing 'Amazing Grace, how sweet the sound,' **the pair of fools.**

Did the lonely man with camera who spent the last sixteen years sneaking about campsites to photo the red bottom baboon monster feeding in a trash can click his shot then run like hell, no, the group of musical pitches and rhythms of the female voice froze him, **the photogenic fool.**

Did the red bottom baboon of lagend seeing the photographer freeze or jump on the photographer and haul him away never to be seen again, or just freeze too listening to the sweet female piece of music, the **red bottom baboon fools.**

Did the kid in the baseball game hit the incoming ball spinning towards him at 90 m.p.h., no he froze as the female voice combined pitch and high notes in a lethal melody, **the athletic fool.**

"Those voices again, I definitely need a shrink," our sheriff but stuffed his ears with chewing gum, but the melody wanted especially him to listen, **the sheriff fool** and he did but at the wrong time for he as Sherlocks Holmes was holding a magnifying glass over Madam Wendy Lou's bed. A hot table light he held in his other hand and was wondering who the black hair, red hair and brown hair belonged to, he suspected Clay, Wendy Lou, and him, then found BLOND HAIRS and stopped thinking so was swallowed up in a melodious female sing-a-long that wanted him to follow the medieval tune, the **fool.**

"I hear my spirit guides of the **dark woods**," Clay Elk hearing the female jingle and stopped his police patrol car to leap out so he could strip down to his beaver pawed print gold 'Y' pants and chant Native American Indian melodies to nature, **the Deputy lawman fool** as he played a flute.

And as the notes drifted into the kitchen window, Mother Cindy Lou heard while drying wet Sunday best China, with wet soapy hands, in scalding water, using lemon juice in her Mr. Sparkle Dish Washer Fluid, **the female fool** as was asking for third degree burns.

"I sang so the fools could hear and help me but instead," and cried, the owner of the charmed melody and the forest acritters stopped following and singing her melody and cried to, "Boohoo," they went.

Instead, Mother Cindy Lou thinking she recognized her daughter's voice burst into joyful tears while waving praises to the Lord Sweet Jesus and thanks to Medium Wendy Lou, threw her best China against kitchen walls and her husband come to investigate the happiness and the lazy dog covered in tobacco stains and the cat seeking revenge for tobacco stains on the kitchen windowsill, knocked them all to six.

Instead, mamma grizzly escaped leaving six testerone filled male grizzlies looking at each other and remembered goldilocks so terrorized camp sites looking for her, and the porridge.

Instead, the cougar found no trace of the wise skunk who had taken the opportunity to vanish. So, a bad-tempered cougar went into Colville River City and shredded washing, knocked over trash cans, nipped into a butchers and left with a prized T Bone Steak reserved for the mayor, and made it to the **dark woods** as weapons is banned in town, so was not shot to pieces, and stuck up as a trophy in Joe's Pub.

Instead, the skunk came to town to and scented all over school as peanut butter jam sandwiches was partial to, but was Saturday and no kids, why is scented in nastiness.

Instead, the beaver failed to plug the hole in the dam and the dam collapsed and sent the beaver a mile downstream so missed the illegal beaver traps.

Instead of catching beaver the illegal trappers in a dance of bad frustration stood in their own sixteen traps and fell into the torrent of water and swept away out of Alaska, and maybe to hell.

Instead of having Big Foot as a trophy the monster hunter, just like that Big Foot did not vanish but appeared in his personnel space, so even his swallowing slow did not save him and he was never seen again, and why Big Foot will never be caught, they are fast footed critters, and fast eaters, not a crumb left.

Instead, a lonely camera was found near a campsite and used up by prankish kids, so when Sheriff Nathan Bottom retrieved it from those delinquent kids and handed it to the chemist for development, no one believed the snaps of the red baboon with mouth wide open, teeth about to snap, as put down to them prankish delinquent kids, and the camera owner was never seen again, and why those red baboons remain as mysterious as the loch Ness Monster.

Instead of trusting Clay when Madam Wendy Lou was involved, Sheriff Bottom screamed as the hot lamp became too hot to hold and it rolled amongst the bedsheets, setting them on fire.

"Sh*t what have I down, I am out of here," and jumped out a closed window, landed headfirst but his soft big ten-gallon sheriff cowboy hat took the fall, then he got up and grabbed a garden hose and turned it on and soaked the whole of Wendy Lou's bedroom, then cleared off before he was discovered, and temptation tempted him to drop a spare deputy badge under the window pointing blame at Clay.

DID HE, was he fink enough?

And as Sheriff Bottom vanished Wendy Lou entered her home from the front door with a client for teacup reading, smelt smoke and noticed a trail of water seeping out her bedroom door.

Sheriff Bottom heard a woman scream just before she fainted.

Sheriff bottom could now be found sitting in his washed, polished hand dried police patrol vehicle, all down by the town drunk, anything done for a drink.

Reading 'Wyatt Earp.'

"This yours," and Madam Wendy Lou tossed in a sheriff badge.

Bottom checked his shirt and found his badge was missing, "titter," the idiot went when he should have vroomed his V8 engine and skedaddled.

"Here is the bill for redecorating and will take more than

Moby Dick to get back under my burnt wet SHEETS, SHERIFF NATHAN BOTTOM," and let an invoice drift onto his crutch.

'PAID,' was stamped on it, also $1000, "reimburse understand or no more goodies."

Sheriff Bottom handed over his credit card that disappeared with Madam Wendy Lou.

Instead of looking before leaping out of a patrol car to dance to Mother Earth, Clay Eagle paid for not doing that, as he leapt down a hundred-foot embankment but was seen several hours later cut and bruised and about to need a doctor as had met poison ivy, 'Oh GAWD,' then the bees that stung him, that Skunk returning home crossed his path and scented him, then that beaver knackered from trekking home whacked him good with her tail, as was in a foul mood.

Then that cougar chased him into town and why he was running in beaver print gold 'Y' pants as never had time to get into his patrol car.

"Help, a cougar wants to eat me, help," he screamed but us good Alaskans keep to our own business so sat in our rocking chairs, smoked weed, ate gobbler burgers, drank a bottle of moonshine, peeked out the privy window, to watch Clay Eagle running and all noticed apart from Clay Eagle as was busy, a massive furry creature nipping amongst the knocked over trash cans a cougar done.

"He always wanted to be close to nature," Mother Cindy Lou polishing the church brass door handles and like the rest of town ignored Big Foot as unlike the rest of the world, did not need a Big Foot trophy to realize the animal existed, why it was risking the runs eating day old half eaten burgers and meat balls in trash cans and spaghetti strings as liked to suck them up through the lips as then the tomato sauce built up, delicious Big Foot knew, worth the runs, there was plenty alleys and your gardens to use in an emergency.

And if you left Big Foot alone, it left you alone, and why Mother Cindy Lou was not stolen and taken into the woods.

Yes, Big Foot was not as blind as we think for Mother Cindy Lou was an elderly person who smoked a clay pipe and chewed tobacco as 'I am a frontiers woman I be,' and spat the tobacco juice out to smolder a cat, smoldering for vengeance after being spat on for years.

Question is, why did not the smoldering cat move, because **it was a fool**.

Instead, Sheriff Bottom did not swallow a bottle of tranquilizers the vet left in case he needed them in the **dark woods** seeking Cindy Lou, 'as strange beasts live in the Alaskan Triangle,' the vet, and the sheriff listened to the charming female notes and drove into the back **dark wood**s of Alaska never to be seen again, fat chance, this is our hero.

"And I kept singing to lure Sheriff Bottom to me," the siren singer surrounded by shipwrecked cars of those that came.

I was sixty miles from him, just ignore the silent radio sheriff and keep coming. I am so lonely and cold, I need a blanket and the central heating upped, logs thrown on the fire, and a gobbler burger, fries and coke, hurry sheriff as am so tired," and the melody ended as the singer exhausted from singing fell asleep, so did the forest critters.

"Where am I?" Sheriff Nathan Bottom pulling into a logging truck lay by and listened again to the female voice in his ears, well he did turn on his V8 and skedaddles to show himself he was a man and 'no woman's door mat,' and explains why he was in a logging truck lay by being an idiot as looks like no one in Colville City is going to vote the man sheriff ever again.

He could go to Hades.

"Sheriff, I am your guide Joseph, a Polish immigrant."

"The voices again, where is my shooter to end it all," Sheriff Bottom and raked in his glove compartment, disentangled unwrapped condoms, unused, sticky ice cream soda chewing gum, brill cream as someone forgot to put the lid back on, "Blast Clay," and took out a vet's tranquilizer gun and held it to his left temple.

"Calm down sheriff Bottom, I am here to help you find the melodious singer and solve this murder case, and by the way, the brill cream is yours," Joseph.

"Get lost," Bottom's reply.

"I am your other guide, a girl sheriff with long legs and Clay uses lots of brill cream in his shiny black hair," and added, *"Fili Pek, get lost."*

[CHAPTER 3] — A KILLER ABOUT

What huge feet Mr. Big Foot

And outside this cave was a pile of rubbish littering the entrance, a sure give away something was living nearby, yes four cheese pizza slices, gobbler burgers with huge bite marks, empty alcohol bottles and squashed tins as the drinkers imitated humans who to show off their strength, crushed a can. Empty bras and panties stolen from washing lines left about, the thieves imitating what they saw happen at Little Joes. All too small for the thieves anyway, just like the cigar butts gathered and lit in a campfire here, yes the thieves here had it good, wine, cigars and floozy whatever's lived here, and if you added the female melodious song, then wine, floozy whatever's, cigars and **song.**

Add the moldy food and the whatever's were living The High Life.

Song Sparrows, Varied Thrush and American Pipit sang remembering the female melody just stopped.

A rich natural imitation as a Great Horned Owl provided bass, and high above a Peregrine Falcon higher notes.

A Common Raven the pitch.

Dozens of Wood Frogs and Pacific Chorus Frog the rhythm.

Inside the cave that smelt of manure a body lay amongst ferns, leaves and the manure that provided heat as it rotted, and ventilation was needed as the stink was phew.

Just where did the whatever's get an idea for a hole filled with yuck, well, Colville City's fantastic sewer system for one.

All was not dark as reddish eyes glowed watching the entrance, waiting for an arrival not yet arrived.

Who could it be?

A five fingered huge hand holding a stick went out to prod the lying body. There was fur on the hand and because of the hand size the owner must be size twenty-six trainers if it had trainers on.

More prodding, no effect, no more sing song melody.

Had the mean idiotic beast prodded to hard and killed the melody singer.

The forest critters fainted with dispair, **the fools**, as these furry monsters came out and collected them that fell on the ground and, ATE THEM, raw.

Anway, the beastly hand went back to eating something, a hand, a smaller hand and was obviously human.

Where was the singer, was it that one under the stinky stuff prodded, or was it ONE OF THOSE THROWN AT THE CAVE BACK, or the owner of those fingers being eaten in old Burritos.

"I have no idea as the stink puts of any investigative guide, I think Sheriff Bottom better take over up here, but not Clay, he is to delicate and the household usage smells did cling to him keeping him away from me, Sheriff Bottom, it was his job as sheriff to become stinky, titter, giggle" Betty Lou, *"the guide with the long shaven female legs."*

There were spirits in this cave, angry, confused, vengeful, wishing when alive they had listened to Granny's Advice, the Girl Friend's, even the Wife's, the boyfriend, the kid, the dog holding your trouser leg, the dog that was not your best friend as when seen what had killed you bolted, smart dog and as Sheriff Nathan Bottom or Clay Eagle were not Doctor Doolittle's, never understood "Woof gr bark woof" meant psychopathic monster got him, and "Mumm," not going back so do not ask me to take you to the idiot master's last place.

But there was innocence too, that had brought nature to the cave entrance to the annoyance of those that lived inside.

Brains these cave squatters had, they had and did figure out why whom and what they must do to get rid of nature's choir outside before it brought that idiot Sheriff Nathan Bottom here, and that handsome native American Deputy who must be six feet.

I am just biased for tall dark mysterious lawmen with colt six shooters strapped to the hips and biased enough to ignore my reason for being a guide, HIM, the squirt under the ten-gallon soft khaki felt hat with a giant star pinned to the middle.

I better shape up, putting to much confidence in my wiggle and see what the bottom under the hat needs?

"Ah look, the ugly monsters coughed up the little song birds as the feathers stuck in their craw, and with a shake, hop and flap, the birdies were safe amongst the pine needles, to sing melody."

*

And way below that idiot Sheriff Nathan Bottom was listening to his guides for once, as he was in the **dark woods** of Alaska, remembering were-wolf stories, thanks to his deputy retelling tales of his tribes 'Shape Changer tales and other monsters eating you that lived here.

Yes, the sun was cloudy as there are about nine sunny days in this part of Alaska and they been used up.

Bottom checked his fuel gauge, about half, which was a relief, and checked his guns, a tranquilizing vet pistol and vet rifle. Yes, he listened too much to his green minded deputy who had indoctrinated him with Native American thinking of respect the land.

He also read the back of major cereal packs while having

breakfast, lunch, and diner, unless he was at Madam Wendy Lou's who feeling sorry, gave him her and Deputy Clay Eagle's leftovers from the back of the fridge, livened up with refried Texan beans, Sheriff Bottom was a lucky human and lucky for others he worked mostly alone as was now full of gaseous nitrogen.

"The more you eat the more you F**t, titter, we girls knew about beans in my time, that no decent girl ate them because, the more you eat the more you F**t, and the gas did build up under your skirts and pleats and before long you were flashing elastic line, giggle."

"I cannot be the only off-guide listening to HER," Joseph and then: "NOW JOSEPH says to our idiot, *"Better hope no red baboon troop visits you with your toys?"* Proving he was the only off-guide present, an unthinking entity energy ball of light with horrid translucent hairy spindly legs that did win him no Boss Angel affection, but do not know about Number Two as what angel answers to, "Oh Number Two were art thou, oh sorry, still in the outhouse doing number twos, giggle, snigger, chuckle, laugh," so was surprised when a bolt of light singed my bum. *"What had I done wrong, maybe the angels were aiming for Joseph and missed, yeh, that was it."*

"Never miss gorgeous," and was Boss Angel so put on my thinking cap and thought, BLANK.

Anyway, the sheriff was seeing red baboons everywhere, even in the back seats where he found evidence, a moldy eaten gobbler burger and a woman's hair grip, a cigar but a wooden carving of Tonka, just what was happening in his patrol car when he was not about, in the bath playing with sailboats and washing Teddy and was called 'TED?
BUT ANYWAY, "Who said that red baboons are here abouts? I demand you show yourself," Sheriff Bottom and so Joseph

kindly did.

"Jesus Chris a blooming ghost," the sheriff's response as he sat grim faced half in his patrol car? The evidence said three people were here, past, not present, maybe future but any suspicions who they were vanished as he swore a red baboon pressed it's face on a side window, and he was half out the patrol vehicle beckoning to be eaten, and never seen again, **"Hallelujah."**

"He is the ugly one, I am Betty Lou the pretty guide, hello sheriff," Betty Lou waving a ghostly transparent hand.

"Jesus Chris another blooming ghost," yes his response.

"We are here to help you; we will show you dead Baldy Pete, also known as Queer Pete, if you let us," Joseph in an unfriendly voice as still not warmed to his assignment, *"he got murdered by the murderer that you got to find Sheriff."*

He did have preferred helping Clay Eagle, who reminded him of a son he never had, handsome, tall, popular, smart at everything and *"Never met Clay Eagle titter,"* as pretty girl guides must titter to show they are not smarter than males.

And Nathan radioed Clay to come join him as he saw Johnny Christy up here a week ago, and did not want to say, "Hi Clay, a ghost told me to start walking, come join me at Mormons Resting Place, which was the truck lay by I was in, and named such as over a hundred years ago a group of Mormon settlers tried to settle in Colville, and failed as central heating was not available back then, a Bottom joke," *"we all got to laugh, titter,"* Betty Lou.

The sheriff started walking back to town laughing aloud as

he had heard "tittering, sniggering, laughing, chuckling," in his head.

"Yeh I was laughing, why walk when you had a patrol vehicle to ride home in luxury."

"Keep walking sheriff the other way and follow the melody and you will find, do not know, but been told to tell you that, and why is he walking when he has a police patrol car with a V8 engine?" Joseph knowing the sheriff was not comparable to his hero Clay Elk.

"Yeh why, oh sheriff why are you walking because you are a FINK?" And the sheriff started running and was obvious now why he was not in the patrol vehicle with that powerful V8 engine waiting to roar down the **dark woods** and make all the sweet songbirds fly south.

It was our fault, the sheriff was clearing his head and knocking it against a nearby Cedar as D.I.Y. exorcism was not working, also that red bum baboon was no longer content looking into his vehicle from the outside, it was now looking from the inside.

If he bashed harder he did be our side and we guides could be off this bad assignment.

"Oh, Sweet Jesus," Betty Lou trying to imitate the ghostly melody we all heard earlier, but **instead,** a moose ran out of the trees and somersaulted Bottom so he landed on his ten-gallon cowboy hat so was p***ed off and the happy mouse headed down towards town.

Instead, a bunch of escaped circus wolves jumped out the trees and pulled from his pockets chili meatball sandwiches, layered in gherkins, layered in cheese slices in a garlic and sesame bun, he had six of them stuffed in his pockets, doing sheriff work was a lonely job in the **dark woods**, and sandwiches could save your live, and did, the six wolves ate them and not him, and headed towards town where after eating that rubbish did foul the streets.

Then an elk, biggest ever with twelve-foot antler span easy **instead** of hiding followed the wolves but paused to head butt Sheriff Bottom as he looked like a hunter in that depressed squashed ten-gallon cowboy hat and boots, so the sheriff was walking unconscious. And the happy elk terrified the town to give it 'The Last Frontier tourist appeal.'

Lucky Bottom, there was no thousand-foot ravine drop nearby, and **instead** of going to roost, a hundred woodpeckers representing all Alaska's eight species flew towards town smelling wood houses to peck for termites as was hungry birds, and saw this figure below with outstretched branches, was his limbs, a walking tree, as was him, so had a rest from flying, on him, in turns as there were a lot of woodpeckers, and each pecked the sh*t out of his hat, and him and left white sh*t on him, but where a happy eight hundred woodpeckers as all felt lighter from pooping so flew quicker into town to peck loudly.

And that stinky skunk **instead** of having enough of humans desiring the quiet life now, ran between Bottom's bottom scenting.

"Oh, Jesus Christ a blooming skunk," the sheriff stinking, "Madam Wendy Lou will not let me sit on her bed sheets and read her bedtime stories such as Moby Dick and Play Girl Magazines as I stink places, darn stinky varmint skunk," *"and he did smell worse than Fili Pek, giggle."*

And the happy skunk was reminded by the sheriff's presence delicious diners could be found in town, so went back to town to stink the place up, and as it left Bottom gave him a squirt for luck.

"My eyes, I am blinded," so walked about lost in the **DARK WOODS** were Big Foot lives.

Then that cougar seeing an easy meal **instead** of being afraid of humans, landed atop the patrol cars roof denting the thin metal roof which reminded Bottom he had a car and why was he walking in tight fitting cowboy boots that was lacerating his heels?

"Jesus Christ I am dead," the sheriff seeing the cougar rushing to greet him, to hug and lick dinner, so our sheriff scrambled up a tree and stayed there. Here the sheriff asked himself why he was walking and blamed that male guide with no name for driving him insane.

"*Call me Joseph sheriff,*" a humble reply as Joseph had been ordered to get the sheriff going the other way to the source of the melody.

"*Should have suggested driving and not walking fool,*" Betty Lou knowing she was pretty and a girl familiar got away with rudeness.

"Wheeze, what you doing up that tree sheriff," Clay asked breathless having run from town believing a cougar was behind him when in fact had overtaken him and was atop the sheriff's patrol car in ambush for Clay Eagle.

"Over there," Sheriff Bottom pointed.

"Heck I need Mounties to get me out of this fix," Clay as he full of adrenalin he thought had used up on the run, joined Sheriff Bottom.

"Where is your shirt Clay, passing folk will think we are strange men doing funny stuff up a tree, maybe mistakenly shoot us as red baboons also, and let us hope we do not meet any up this tree," the sheriff added wisely.

"Shame, Clay is cold, I will warm him," Betty Lou and wrapped warm loving spirit energy about Clay who began to snooze off.

"Blooming heck those ghosts have possessed Clay," the sheriff seeing the cougar vamoose towards town were dropped pizza slices waited to be eaten, and the droppers, so was a happy cougar. And Bottom began to clamber down the tree when sad tuneful notes of a mouth organ drifted to him and cigar smoke and was sure he saw a sombrero over that cougar and a shadowy figure stroking the cat when he should have been eaten.

"It is that unemployed vagrant I keep forgetting to kick out of town," Sheriff Bottom who had good eyesight as had a driving license.

The sheriff searched for a gun forgetting the tranquilizers weapons where in the patrol car.

On the ground he picked up a solid tree branch to defend Johnny Christy from feeding that cougar with himself. Above him Clay sound asleep from an exhausting run slid off the branch and landed on our sheriff.

"PLUNK."

That is why with no little coaching from his guides, *"Get up, no sleeping on the job, follow the music,"* did sheriff Bottom not get up as both me and Fili Pek were shouting, loudly in his head.

"Oh hello, who are you?" Me Betty Lou who is telling this story from here on asked another guide, a fearsome Native American with rattle snake rattlers all over him, *"rattling."*

"Rattling Snake, Clay's Native American Guide."

"I do not believe this," Joseph afraid his angel helpers did appear in a thunderclap, as Betty Lou flirted.

"I hate snakes, hate them, loathe them, Fili Pek remove him from my presence."

And the Fili Pek answer was maniacal laughter.

AND the mouth organ music faded *and was he eaten down the road?*

And what happened to that red baboon in the patrol vehicle, well that cougar had an extended belly, was she a pregant cougar or full of baboon, but why she never ate Johnny Christy? There was no room in her belly.

He also carried vials of cat nip in pockets in his sombrero

*

And a big shadow fell across the two lawmen who were lying atop each other in a strange position that had their moons pointing to the heavens.

The sound of a cutthroat razor opening alerted Sheriff Bottom to his danger.

"Well Betty Lou, you going to tell why the sheriff knew what sound a cutthroat razor made upon opening?" Joseph asked.

"Why silly, all Alaskan know to keep a cutthroat razor handy as electricity is haphazard in winter, and why I kept a small pink one stuffed in my elastics, just in case someone like you gets to eager Joseph," me telling him, when in truth no woman liked to show off hairy legs when those nine days of Alaskan sunshine happened, shorts and thermal bikini time.

"Grunt," Sheriff Bottom wishing he were not the bottom of the two law men, try as he might he could not ease himself up to see who was standing above them.

"Guess you are not that COUGAR as got red mountain boots on," the sheriff noticing all the detail on the lower feet of his what, assailant or rescuer, murderer?

"Going to scalp this Native American and then you, pity about the Indian, handsome boy, think will come back with a pickup and taxidermist him into a panty holder in one hand, and a weed ash tray in the other.
I had a taxidermist stuffed cat but it escaped.
Keep the deputy other places as a furry hat holder," and Moriarty laughter and I kicked him a place, but my spiritual kick was pushed upside down, so I tumbled into the Ether by his dark spiritual guides, **dark wood** imps.

"Hey, who are you whatever you are try me, I am tougher?" Joseph but was outnumbered by dark imps giving bad advice to the stranger on his shoulder such as:

"Throw the sheriff into the cave, the squatters will thank you by leaving you alone," one dark imp.

"No, take him home and turn him into a French maid, titter," another more stupid dark imp.

"No, use the razor places now, giggle," a gormless dangerous dark imp.

"Better work him over before moving Clay off him, these lawmen are armed and dangerous," an extremely nasty thinking dark imp.

"The sheriff never carries a gun," Joseph protested.

"Well done idiot," I called to him.

Then the sound of a million rattle snakes as Clay's Rattling Snake guide tried to scare the imps away, almost worked as they fell silent fearing the snake out of the Bible was near, thus giving mankind and imps a fear of snakes, well most are not venomous, but those that rattle are.

"Turn round and kick out Sheriff," I screamed in his right ear.

"Roll sideways sheriff and keep rolling," Joseph shouted in the sheriffs other ear.

"It was a sheriff with tinnitus and Epley balance problems that rolled staggered got up staggered and was pushed down and clubbed so that was the end of his rescue effort," Betty Lou.

"Will not scalp him, where is my chloroform for emergencies such as this," the stranger and out of a canvas male shoulder bag, popular in male fashion these days, he found the chloroform and sprinkled lots onto Clay's face.

"Puff," Rattling Snake causing a slight breeze to blow the doping liquid away.

"Help," I screamed at the top of my spirit energy.

"You called," and was the angels of Joseph, *"Not the lawmen time to go home,"* and the looney with the razor succeeded in cutting his left thumb.

The dark imps hissed and imitated rattler rattles, but we were wise to that trick.

Then the sound of a mouth organ playing a funeral march from the woods.

The strange man living up to the reputation of 'STRANGE MAN' closed his cutthroat looking towards a commotion coming up the road from town.

"That is the way sheriff, punch him again and kick him places," I shouted in eagerness as our sheriff attacked.

Thing is, Sheriff Bottom was about four six and this strange man over six feet.

It could have been ugly for Bottom, but chloroform was scattered in his face, and that is why sheriffs have deputies for a soft landing.

The man ran up the road shouting back, "I will not forget," and added so none heard, "I need stitches," as not only had he cut himself with his razor but done it again upon closing the cutthroat.

"Look Big Foot," someone in the commotion coming up the road and bird shot was fired.

"Sh*t," the strange man adding, "I need these pellets pulled out of my bum," and then was round the bend and starting **a V8 purple pickup with a skull crest on the doors and escaped.**

"Big Foot can drive," another in the commotion hearing the engine roar away.

*

"Revenge was is on my mind, Colville City is going to pay for that buckshot," the idiot behind the wheel as he was already making the city pay.

And the strange man was about to play for playing with sharp razors, for his steering wheel was getting slippery and them back roads are full of potholes, and why 4x4's are driven, but it could be a tank, you need dry hands, not hands covered in red congealing fluid, that stretched to his itchy nose and scratchy crutch, and dripped to his feet on the pedals.

Lucky it was an automatic.

Then the red baboons attracted by the smell of blood from a mile away arrived.

They travel fast these apes through the treetops silently.

Otherwise, the town mob did hear them and sober up and go home.

"Splat," the sound of red baboon turd hitting his windscreen.

Followed by more splats as the apes wanted him to stop and make the mistake of getting out to see if he was seeing what his eyes told him he was seeing on his windscreen.

It certainly smelt so.

Then the red baboons did be noisy as they flocked him with those human fingers and big fangs.

And he did be seen no more, and as the red baboons have opposing thumbs, they can steer the 4x4 and since the engine is on, one presses the accelerator pedal and the vehicle disappears into the bush, never to be seen again as it rusts away as oxidising wins.

Those red baboons know all this as watch their human neighbors.

So, steal like bears do from picnic spots, by appearing making chatter to terrorize the humans into fleeing.

Plenty to eat on the picnic tables.

Gobbler burger in mayo.

Gobbler burger and ketchup.

Curried gobbler burger.

Pumpkin pie and chocolate cream.

Chocolate brownies.

Alcoholic drinks.

And if lucky, a radio with working batteries.

And the red baboons partied.

Eating, drinking, dancing, fighting, even murdering their own over a floozy red baboon on heat.

Yes, those red baboons were human.

But they were dealing with the strange man whom by experience knew always escaped. Just maybe this time he did screw up and get out.

He also had nasty weapons and although the red baboons never buried their fallen, knew where he had killed them.

That shaded spot under the Alaskan Pine where toadstools grew now fed and nourished by the fallen.

And the fallen bodies were never discovered by towns folk as the wolves, bears, cougars, and squirrels ate the rest, so were so well fed never ate any one when wandering sight seeing in Colville City.

"Home at last, now for band aid," the strange man arriving at his log cabin and there in the shadows, **a Big Foot, many Big Foot, and the red baboons ran away towards picnic sites.**

"Garble," a Big Foot, *"Oh dear it was a girl and just asked the strange man to marry her, giggle, got to see this, chuckle."*

"Garble," the strange man replied shaking his head and went into his log cabin garage where he opened a freezer and took out a bag of frozen lamb chops, went outside and the Big Foot sensing feeding time showed themselves.

At least a dozen, black, brown, red in color and some rubbing their tummies.

Out came the cut-throat, the Big Foot retreated, the man who fed them was still an untrustworthy human.

He slit open the bag and threw the lamb chops at the ape men, and noticed he threw a little finger also.
Stifling a curse, he went into the house and got his band aid.

Which was useless for an amputated finger.

"Where is that finger," and looked out the window and watched that girl Big Foot tilt it's head back and drop his finger down its throat.

"I need to get medical help, I will pay back my pain on them lawmakers and Colville City," and laughed and the Big Foot imitated him thinking that is what humans do after a feed.

And he drove his 4x4 away.

In the open back he heard strange 'cooing' sounds and looking in the mirror saw big lips kissing the back glass.

It was her, the girl ape not giving up on marriage.

Then she put her fist through the glass and smeared her dung all over his head, neck, shoulders, back and since they got big hairy arms down his moon, she was scenting him, making sure no other Big Foot female got to close to HER HUMAN.

"Ooooh," the strange man as that ape got places on his moon so he drove off the mountain road and the girl Big Foot did not want to die, so leaped to safety.

As for stinky in the 4x4 the pickup thundered onto the road below, hubcaps span away, a suspension on a rear wheel went and the shock wave of hitting the road below cracked his front driver window.

The shock of impact also forced his breakfast and lunch out of him.

"Bl***y monkey," and lucky for him that girl ape never heard him or did take offence at being called a monkey. "Going to cost me a fortune, need to go into Canada and rob Native American Settlements and nip back to Alaska and a mobster garage."

He because of how handsome Clay Eagle was, had Native Americans on his brain.

Did he ever think as people some were tall and lanky with acne.

Did he ever think as people some were shrimps like Sheriff Bottom.

Did he ever think as people some were brainy and worked in cities.

Did he ever think as people some were loaded working in the casinos.

Yes, he did and why he was coming 'a choo chugging puffing round the bend, hoot, hoot.'

And somewhere before driving through the meadows and not through the boarder check point, as that is what 4x4 are about, he better jump in a freezing river and clean up, as did he stink of s**t.

*

"I had to drive into British Columbia to get those pellets removed by a trans call night worker and the pain was delightful," even got her to stitch my thumb up and she did as on the motel bedside table a wad of dollars.

She made some phone calls and a knock on the door; it was an expensive little finger made of wood with springs where the knuckles had been.

In the morning we left together and as the sun was not properly up made an excuse about being aroused and drove into a side road.

In the back of my truck Big Foot rubber shoes, a cheese wire, and a 'Do It Your Self Jack The Ripper Beginners Tool Kit.'

Got my money back and drove away with no passenger.

And unknown to the strange man the 'Delivero' 'Just Eats' boy who dropped off the prosthetic little finger, was a good friend of the missing trans medic street walker.

"He drives a purple 4x4 pick up with a skull crest on the doors, is Alaskan number plates that even tell me where in Alaska he lives, Colville City, you're a dead strange man if my trans medic street walker never shows again.

Right know I am giving you the benefit of belief, let us believe my trans friend went to holiday with you, of course at a daily fee.

Then the police found the body and the delivery boy was heartbroken.

There were big footprints about the scene.

"Big Foot got her," a tall handsome Mounty.

And in the glove compartment of the getaway vehicle, blood-stained green panties, a souvenir, and the strange man better hope he never did need a trans street walker medic again, and the way he open and closed that razor, the odds were in favor of needing one.

"Oh well, Tar La Lee, it goes."

*

"Who killed my daughter Cindy Lou?" Mother Cindy Lo asked Wendy Lou the medium.

"A pervert," Wendy Lou replied.

"You mean Johnny Christy, I knew it," Mother Cindy Lou and Father Cindy Lou fingered the colt in his pocket, as he wore big baggy trousers made for hiding colt firearms in.

"No Johnny Christy is straight, better be," Wendy Lou let that slip.

The parents of Cindy Lou stared her out figuring the medium knew more than willing to talk.

Father Cindy Lou clicked the safety off on his colt pistol.

Medium Wendy Lou looked at him recognizing the sound, these were frontiers folk as Alaska was still one of the unexplored wildernesses of the world.

"He brings his washing here and baby sits," Medium Wendy Lou truthfully and clicked the safety of her derringer.

"Yeh, we heard you got four kids, unmarried too," Mother Cindy Lou making enemies.

"I ask him to look after my cat, you know the one that sneaks into your house," Medium Wendy Lou reminding all her cat was a sadist vengeful animal that did harm to those that harmed her.

"Yeh, I know of the beast," Mother Cindy Lou holding up her bandaged hands for the cat was a savage beasty and Mother Cindy Lou looked about for a spittoon for her tobacco spit, found none and swallowed.

Why her bandaged hands clutched her throat and then one on her husband's right leg and squeezed something as Mother Cindy Lou gagged.

A gun shot ran out and Father Cindy Lou got up holding his right leg and hobbled out the door.

Medium Wendy Lou scooped up the twenty dollars just in case a refund was asked, as Mother Cindy Lou gagged her way out the house too.

For good measure, a vengeful cat jumped on her back.

"Oh, Sweet Jesus Lord save me demons are on me," and Mother Cindy Lou knew The Lord was punishing her for visiting a medium rather than trusting in HIM and the cousins and uncles, aunts, nieces, and nephews that made up a lynching mob in finding that murderer of Cindy Lou.

And the wise cat left her and hid in the shadows of a sidewalk as Mother Cindy Lou looked for demons and saw none.

Inside a house, Medium Wendy Lou opened a woman's fashion catalogue and decided she could buy that sexy cat woman outfit for when johnny Christy visited with his laundry AGAIN.

She went to work ordering on her laptop, and even had enough for special delivery.

Johnny Christy if he were not the ones playing in the **dark woods** with a strange man would be the luckiest man in Colville City when that cat outfit arrived.

And where was Johnny Christy, standing over two hapless lawmen and how did he get there, **it was a secret.**

"Look at these two 'Thai Lady Boys,' Mother Cindy Lou being mean standing over the lawmen also and how did she get there, on a broom stick, **no it was a secret.**

"*And how does she know about Thai Lady Boys?*" I asked but as a spirit guide was not heard.

"*They gave a show in Fair Banks,*" Joseph and all us spirits looked at him strangely and added, "*Oh yeh, tell us more,*" and he did.

Now Johnny Christy dragged the lawmen separately to the police patrol vehicle and dumped them in.

They were atop each other again.

"Click," repeatedly as Mother Cindy Lou used her Polaroid. It was bigger than her shoulder bag, where did she get it, did she say a spell, **no it was her secret.**

And as the sounds of an angry town mob appeared Johnny got in the car.

"Click," a polaroid and he never asked her how she got ahead of that angry mob and if he did she would never tell him, **it was a secret.**

It was also **a secret** what johnny Cash looked like, no photograph had appeared in newspapers and never would, and just like that a polaroid disappeared.

"Where did it go?" An amazed and then peeved off Mother Cindy Lou and as she swung a right kept swinging as the car was gone.

It was Johnny Christy' **secret** how he got the polaroid and **would remain a secret.**

Now expertly he drove the vehicle in reverse through that mob, not knocking over a single man, woman, elk, or child.

Then noticed Mother Cindy Lou spread across the front windscreen, how did she get there, **it was her secret.**

That is why cars have a water spray and wipers and he wiped her away.

And did it without mordaciously biting his lips and with his sombrero pulled down to his nose, and cigar smoke filling his eyes, and explains why he missed the lot as he roared the V8 engine off the road and the car sailed again in clean Alaskan air.

"We been cheated boy," a leader of the pack, puffed on weed, guzzled moonshine and "Come on boys, let us get them," and the crowd of two hundred sauntered down the road to Colville City, slowing down as weed and moonshine and under cooked gobbler burgers took effect.

Behind a haze of weed drifted towards a picnic area and

soon a troop of red bottom baboons was happy, not a murderous thought amongst them as rivals went off to the **dark woods** with girl baboons and girls with boy red bum baboons.

They was spaced out to hell.

And the police patrol car landed on the church roof making a hole, but the vehicle was intact as the roof took the fall, and the boys someone inside the vehicle pushed them out, so they rolled down the church roof into horse troughs full of cold freezing drowned mosquito water.

And the lawmen awoke huddled together.

"Best we vamoose before we are seen together again Clay," Sheriff Bottom and ran from alleyway to alleyway to his jail and dry clothes and a spare ten galloon hat with a sheriff badge on it.

Clay watched the patrol vehicle rush out the church front door with the door stuck in the front bumper and disappear behind the jail.

He heard mouth organ music in the police patrol vehicle.

He heard banjo strumming when the police vehicle stopped.

He smelled cigar smoke.

He even picked up a cigar butt still glowing and smoked it.

He headed to Madam Wendy Lou for comfort.

"And it was a decent job none had head lice with all this huddling together, titter."

"That is it, your replaced, by me," Number Two but he spoke without authority so was ignored.

*

"Meow," a vengeful, cat likening the cat outfit, thinking Wendy was buying her a playmate to boss.

"Hi baby, wow that looks sexy," Clay having just walked in which was a mistake as a free woman like Medium Madam Wendy Lou might be making cakes with a red baboon, sorry I mean a small little man whose feet can be seen sticking out from under a sheriff's hat.

"You ever knock Clay; I might be in my panties wanting a shower?" Wendy asked and Clay got hot thinking about it as that mosquito cold horse trough water dripped and pooled on Wendy's clean antiseptic floor.

"Oh, Great Tonka," Clay exclaimed as Wendy bent his fingers back leading him to the back door, opened it, pushed him out and he saw lots of other girls half-dressed doing exactly the same as she, teaching the boyfriend he was one of many boyfriends, but they did not know that and that is why they put up with the finger braking routine and put it down to *'that time in the month.'*

Anyway: Father Cindy Lou just happened to be limping quickly through folks backyards to reach the Cottage Hospital to get treated for a gunshot wound in the leg.

He pretended not to look at all the women in their colored panties but the women knew him better and posed with their chests puffed up.

A grin spread across Father Cindy Lou's face; he did have to shot himself more often.

Then all the doors closed and Clay just stood there mouth open speechless, then heard the 'Rattle," so woke up and being a fast draw plastered his space with bullets at a rattler.

"Rattle," went his guide Rattling Snake, "Sheriff Bottom

needs you, hurry, is a life-or-death need."

That made Clay become action man and he bolted for his deputy patrol vehicle which was his own car as them councilors was a mean lot.

"Enaw," went the siren as he sped away observing the 15 m.p.h. City Speed Limit, stopping to let Mother Cindy Lou run past on the way to the Cottage Hospital with Wendy Lou's mangy cat on her back.

The next stoppage was Father Cindy Lou running out a back-alley way holding a rattler that seemed to have bitten his chest, and as Father Cindy Lou passed Clay, Clay saw father throw the tangled snake away, tangled in false 'Austin Powers Bright Red Chest Hair, attached to an inflatable chest that was deflating from a rattler bite.

Clay thought it about time the city did something about the snake problem, like move the city.

The next stoppage was the pastor screaming and throwing bibles, hymn books and prayer books at the police patrol vehicle, Clay ignored him and sped on.

Passing Little Joes, the pub that doubled as a bordello, he was forced to stop again as lingerie floated onto his windscreen obliterating his view, then a woman's body bounced off the windscreen.

"S**t," another homicide.

Then the body hissed away as it deflated in the air.

Then at THUD as a man hit the dirt road in front of the police vehicle.

Clay shook his head in disbelief as a drunk stood up and wondered away in his star and stripe shorts.

"My sheriff needs me, life or death, my siren is on and I am stuck in Colville City as the Lollipop Woman guides the primary school kids to the library. Hellfire I better hurry, that pastor has almost caught me up."

Then gleefully Clay was out of City Limits and started to put his foot down.
The speedo raced up.
"Ride them, round them up, brand them," Clay sang until suddenly when there had been no one there a second ago a man under a sombrero playing a mouth organ stood there.

Clay hit the breaks but there was no 'WHACK.'

"Speed up deputy, a sheriff needs you," and the man sitting next to him played his mouth organ, coughed, spat out a cigar butt and played again.

Clay drove on not asking how Johnny Christy did that illusionist trick, and how did he get into his patrol vehicle, it was **Johnny's secret.**

"Tonka, save me from White Men," Clay prayed and Rattling Snake was a happy Rattling Snake guide.

Then Clay noticed the female panty stuffed in Johnny's pocket, for laundry purposes 'Wendy Lou,' was printed on the purple elastic hem.

Clay began to see red as he had excellent vision.
Rattling Snake wanted to urge him to scalp Johnny.
Clay was confused.

His fingers still ached from the bending.

He remembered all the other folk being led out the back yard with bent fingers.

He was not alone.

That mollified him.

Then Johnny was gone.

A yellow bra with 'Wendy Lou,' for laundry purposes was were Johnny had been sitting.

"He went away with the panties s**t he has been cleaning Madam Wendy Lou's fridge, worse teaching her to play the mouth organ, worse changing strings on his banjo, worse, she has been smelling of cigar lately, and I thought it was my friend Sheriff Bottom who I began to think was not a friend if he could visit MY GIRL **in secret**, but now I know the snake is Johnny Christy, Ch***t he is a tramp full of S.T.D., bubonic plague, T.B., foot and mouth and has passed his diseases to me, I am dead, and where are those panties," and drove over Sheriff Bottom who had got out of his patrol vehicle paid for my Colville City, another point of **animosity, jealousy** between friends.

And because he drove over his ex-friend only heard and felt a thump and as he was looking backwards, saw a sheriff ten-gallon hat spiral away.

Clay's foot came off the speed pedal.

"*You murdered him Clay rattle,*" Rattling Snake happy a 'Whiteman hit the dust.'

Guilt filled Clay as he was guilty of murderous thoughts over Madam Wendy Lou.

"*A pioneer woman Clay, not Native American,*" Rattling Snake was racist, well, it was his memories that sometimes flooded him, of settlers burning down his villages, he moved about a lot to avoid being burned, yes, his present guide job was a healing mission for him and with those sort of remarks Boss Angel would send him to The OUTER DARKNESS where for company, The Wild Bunch, Jessie James, Sundance, Butch Cassidy, The Clanton's, TED, and all White Men except the beer.

Angels way above Boss Angel in their wisdom knew if he hung about Sheriff Bottom did change his views on settlers and become multi racial, happy, content and do his guide job.

"Sheriff Bottom, a wise pick," Betty Lou suppressing a giggle.

And Clay got out and saw a lifeless body under a ten-gallon hat, he had killed Nathan, *"your ex-friend,"* Rattling Snake.

"Hey , Clay stop eyeing up that red baboon I am over here with clues to Cindy Lou," and Clay Eagle recognized his sheriff and looked back and forth repeatedly at the thingmabob he had run over.

"What the hell did I drive over?" He asked.

"Rattle," a useless guide.

And found out, **a stranger appeared** at the edge of the cedar trees waving a football rattle, as his fingers some were gone, and others wrapped in band aid.

It was enough to awaken what was lying under the sheriff's coat and hat.

A bad-tempered red baboon, well it had been run over.

"Tonka C**p," and Clay ran for his patrol vehicle and got in, just in time as these fangs appeared on his side windows dribbling salvia and was obvious what the message was, "You are my dinner."

And the stranger walked over confidently towards Clay forgetting the shrimp under the sheriff hat.

Just as a million red baboons stuck their red bums on Clay's clean windows and made him retch, the sound of a V8 engine.

Whatever sounds red baboons make as they scampered as Sheriff Bottom's patrol vehicle stopped alongside Clay's vehicle.

The sheriff wound down his window when he could have spoken to his deputy on the radio.

"He killed Cindy Lou, get you colt ready," was the sheriff 's last famous words as leaving an open window open **amongst a pack of red baboons directed by an evil stranger** was asking for it.

And a vial of red baboon pheromones dropped out of a strangers pocket, without that he was red baboon dinner, with it HE was THEIR AMHPRODITIES and would never hurt him but bring him grubs, fresh fish unscaled, birds to swallow hole, dried fox pooh as a deliciously, yes he need that vial of PHERMONES or he was a gonna.

And the sheriff got it.

"That is my ex-friend you are eating," and Clay opened his window and fired several times at the stranger, missing every blo****g time.

But as tree bark splintered about the cowardly stranger, he fled as melodious music filled the air.

"He is the one,
Do not be fooled by his looks,

Beauty is skin deep.
All lies, beauty is up front,
So, he got me, him,
Do your job," the squirrels and such repeated till both lawmen nodded repeatedly like Japanese battery toys.

"And my boys did not give chase to the strange man. In their defense The Mannie had gone into the woods with the red baboons. Did they not watch drive in movies were police hard men with bald heads always get their baddy, admittingly after being hit a hundred times with bullets, burned, pushed out of a skyscraper, thrown to sharks, trod over by police horses that weed on them, yes, guess they did watch these movies so explains why they fled, the mealy cowards."

"We need to buy a bazooka off eBay Nathan," best friends again.

"Why is that Clay, friend," the sheriff and was heart wrenching.

"I am out of bullets," Clay which meant they had a vet tranquilizer gun in the sheriff's patrol car, and "where was it?"

Just over there.

"Need to wash it later when you pick it up Sheriff Bottom," no longer friends as the sheriff's vehicle was a mass of red baboon bums pointed at them.

"I will give the town drunk a tenner to collect the vehicle later and then fine him a tenner for driving under the influence of alcohol and then offer him a 'Out of jail' card if he washes my patrol vehicle, and no way **Deputy** am I going over to my vehicle to collect the tranquilizer gun," *"yes, no longer friends as Clay did not want to come back with his friend Nathan to get the vehicle and* *be eaten."*

And the sheriff realized that and that meant they were not friends.

"Hey sheriff it is raining rocks," I shouted at them both as the rocks sounded like heavy hailstones on the vehicle roof.

"Deputy please drive away and we will keep this to ourselves," Sheriff Bottom looking at the many Big Foot creatures throwing rocks and tree branches at them, "and we better buy a bazooka each out of eBay **Deputy.**"

"A right couple of useless lawmen?" Joseph and went as an orb to fly about the Gigantopithecus whatever very tall, hairy, muscular apes in an effort to distract them for 'My Boys' to flee.

"Well done Fili Pek," I added seeing the immigrant in a new light.

"Is that a compliment?" He asked and saw straight away he visualized a romantic fling on far away Saturn, just typical of a male, whether alive or dead, think of one thing, milking the cows at 4 a.m."
"Do not push it FILI PEK, Son of Pen**."
"I really hate that bi***."

"Ouch," Sheriff Bottom who liked an open window. It let the fresh air in, and out the clean washing smell of Clay's laundry that reminded him of who washed Clay's clothes, Madam Wendy Lou.

He also liked the window down as folk could see his whole head and hat blocking the window and think he was big, tough, and armed and 'do not mess with me.'
And think he might be bald like the tough television

lawmen.

"Ouch," this time the stone missed Sheriff Bottom and hit Clay who sagged forward onto the wheel and his foot came off the pedal and the car slowed down.

"S**t, I am going to be eaten alive," Sheriff Bottom as the throwers of the rocks, Big Foot and those red bottom baboons sensing dinner advanced noisily.

It was enough to bring the stranger back, after a ten-minute pause, and he was panting heavily as he must have gone a bit and understanding the excitement of the ALASKAN TRIANGLE MONSTERS sprinted back and seemed in pain as he sorted stuff out in those undersize 'Y' Fronts 6 sizes too small.

Behind him a female Big Foot in love took her time, she knew no human could keep that sprint up for long in 'Y' pants six sizes to small on.

A dangerous thing to do running in thick **dark woods** where tree branches waited to whack you, cut you, give you black eyes and cauliflower ears.

Also rip your clothes and since he was not wearing a shirt to show off his gym work out muscles, was cut a thousand times.

Even his bum was not spared from branches swinging back he had pushed out of the way.
Then he been bit so many times by rattlers was immune, that or he injected daily an anti-venom because there was one hanging onto his zip.

A small baby, cute.

Which upon entering the road clearing he tossed it away.

It **either** landed safely and lived to grow bigger and bite him again.

Or **either** landed amongst the red bum baboons and was torn to shreds and eaten, not getting a chance to bite any as them baboons had learned from watching Grandma Mother Cindy Lou brushing rattlers out of the church hall, especially since there was no front door.

It gets cold in Alaska and them reptiles need to get shelter.

It might have **also** landed inside the patrol vehicle as Sheriff Bottom had the window down.

"I will save you dear," I shouted and Fili Pek cheered but did not mean him, but Clay and used my energy to push down the speed pedal and the car drove off the road and **sailed into the blue sky, again.**

Hitting a red baboon waving a cutthroat razor under Sheriff Nathan's nose and then, "PLOP," a baboon finger lay on Nathan's lap staining his trousers.

He thought of Wendy washing the stains out for as 'if she could wash for him, then she better wash for me.'

And a large human hand covered in band aid took hold of Clay's door handle and opened it.

"Dark imps, what a stink, oh sweetheart Joseph help me please," and was lies and only being nice as needed him.

Then an open cutthroat razor dropped onto Sheriff Bottom's crutch.

He grimaced.

This is when the car sailed off the road.

107

"I am a dead man anyway my will is up to date, I am leaving all to The Colville National Park where my friends live," the strange man whose fingers were leaving the door handle and as he fell away.

"Bye," Clay said as he straightened and, "Tonka receive my soul to the happy hunting grounds," and "rattle," was heard.

"Notice the 'rattle' is not in italics so is not Clay's guide Rattling Snake and where is he, never here when needed."

And Mother Cindy Lou had gotten a lynch mob together to lynch a no-good sheriff and his deputy for the church had collapsed. Seems a lot of structural damage was done when that patrol car smashed violently through the church roof.

Luckily, no shapely Cindy Lou's where about but this time there had been one, an elderly lady with a bent warty nose, and she had her own black cat, and a broom she used to sweep the rattlers out of church.

Yes, Grandma Cindy Lou had been there when the whole church collapsed.

Now the Fire DEPATMENT WAS THERE AND FORMED A HUMAN CHAIN GANG TO REMOVE THE TIMBER PLANKS.
They knew she was alive as she was smoking tobacco and her black cat was sitting above where she had been buried alive.

"Come on folks, here is that sheriff up the road, and I have a necktie, let us go," Mother Cindy Lou and had used the church collection dish to pay many alcoholic drinks for the many drunks in Little Joes.

They wanted a lynching and who better to lynch than that

useless sheriff, and his deputy.

And as Mother Cindy Lou led the lynch mob out of town a shadow drew over them.

"It is the Thunder Bird come to eat us," just takes one to mention a bird of Native American Legend that is so big, well, it does eat you.

"It poohed on me," as a squirrel disturbed from sleep by their noise threw an accurate acorn.

"Where is Big Mike, he is missing, been taken, I am out of here," and takes two.

"I paid good money for your drinks, come back here, there is nothing above us apart from a black cloud," Mother Cindy Lou and waved a pocketbook of Mormon as she got about her churches.

Then Big Mike walked out from behind a tree where he had been watering, looked up and went back behind the tree.

"See, Big Mike is here, come here Big Mike," Mother Cindy Lou screamed just as the police vehicle landed on her.

Then the police vehicle drove away.

"Hello, I am a ghost are you one too?" I asked the depression in the road where a police vehicle had been and where was Mother Cindy Lou, **it was her secret**, maybe the hit had forced her down to Australia, *"giggle."*

"Idiots, there is Mother Cindy Lou," and I looked and there she was with an arm of Johnny Christy on her as he played his mouth organ with the other as he sat in the open boot.

Then the vehicle stopped abruptly at the jail house and the lawmen fled inside.

"Rattle," it was just a baby rattler and out it came, "rattle," defiantly and slid under the jail house, probably looking for a loose wall or floor plank and get into the jail, them Alaskan nights were cold.

And because the patrol vehicle stopped suddenly, Mother Cindy Lou who had been ogling Johnny Christy close up, wishing she could take him home and give her husband leave to live at Little Joes, forever, she was thrown against Johnny and the boot shut.

"Madam, those are my chest hairs," and "I am spoken for," and" help," and for once there was no mouth organ music but plenty movement in the boot so the car bounced this way and that.

The fenders pinged off.

The wheel caps flew off.

The suspension collapsed.

And the pastor stopped to see who had shouted, "help."

"Help," he heard again and did what any upright citizen did do, opened the boot and the boot lid flew open instantly connecting with the pastor's chin.

He lay now as an unconscious churchman, just as well for Mother Cindy Lou.

And Johnny Christy fled the scene.

"I got your 'Y' fronts.

And Madam Wendy Lou watching from a window was not amused, why Johnny, that woman was old enough to be your granny, and Madam Wendy Lou peered good and her face exploded in shock, it was Granny Grandma Cindy Lou, then who was buried back at the church, **it was a secret,** and a black cat ran over and purred at Granny Cindy Lou's feet, and was rewarded with a dried bit of salmon, as Granny Lou spoiled her cat.

*

"Look Clay what we have," and Sheriff Bottom emptied his ten-gallon hat.

The cutthroat razor plunked onto his desk.
Red bum baboon blood oozed from it.
A fly immediately landed on it; flies even get to Alaska.
And Clay dropped a red baboon finger next to the razor.

"We know this strange man, think hard Clay," Sheriff Bottom implying Clay was an imbecile *"as they were no longer best friends over a washer woman, titter, giggle."*

And Clay gave his Boss a blank stare, even I did not know whom the evil stranger was?

And at that moment a lit cigar butt landed on the table splattering hot ash towards the lawmen.

"You going to arrest him, he is wanted in other States for kidnapping, murder and the Mounties in British Columbia want him for the dismemberment of a transexual street walking medic.

"I am on fire Clay, get the fire extinguisher," Sheriff Bottom.

"Get it yourself, I am also on fire."

Then the front door opened and closed and a banjo strummed angrily, then a mouth organ was heard and the sound of a deputy police vehicle driving off.

"Argh," a woman's scream was heard.

"That sounded like I dare say, Mother Cindy Lou Deputy Clay Eagle, go and look please," as the sheriff when ordering was polite.

"Yep, it is her and she is crawling here, maybe we should lock the door and be really quiet as if no one is in.

"Brilliant idea Clay."

Then I saw the cute thing before they heard it, but they did hear Mother Cindy Lou threaten to let Father Cindy Lou shoot the door down, "come out and get lynched," and shouting like that brings a curious crowd, and Little Joe was getting mighty fed up with suddenly losing custom just like that.

"Who is the murderer Sheriff," Clay wanting to know before he was lynched.

"No idea deputy, why?"

And a certain deputy saw RED.

*

And a dark stranger had let go of the door handle as the police vehicle sailed into the sky.

Both feet wobbled on the ridge edge.

He reached his band aid hands back to grab a branch and pull himself to safety.
He felt fur.
He heard Big Foot girl sounds a Big Foot girl sounds when she has found her mate for life.

"I am better off with them lawmen," and left go but she was a wise girl, and held his hands tight, so his sores under the band aid crippled him with pain.

He blanked out, even hard men do, it was the smell, the Big Foot stink that made him loose consciousness, but anyway, he came too bobbing and the soil looked about nine feet down, where was he, and the STINK told him, plus the ribbons he had given her to make a friend and slave out of her.

She had him, she was bigger than him, why those biceps where so close they were enormous. If he got her angry she did pulverize him, it was rumored the YETI ate men's dangly bit.

That part of him tried hard to retreat into his body but no avail, fur was in the way.

Where was she taking him, oh dear other Big Foot were jumping for joy showering the happy couple with branches and stones.
He was knocked unconscious again.
He awoke on a moldy straw bed littered with forest fruits and flowers.
He could see the cave opening.
He was going to make a run for it.

Did he make it or did she suddenly appear with dinner, roast red baboon bum.
Did she find him gone and grunt roar revenge on WHITEMEN.
*"Did she he well titter, it is **a ladies secret**?*

I almost forgot, to let the rest of her tribe know HE was hers, had rubbed him down with her pooh, boy did he stink, but not to the Big Foot, he smelt fine."

CHAPTER 4
VENGEANCE VISITS

Sheriff Nathan Bottom was a small man who did not carry a gun,
So many asked, "How is he still alive?" Perhaps so
small the bullets just zoomed over him.

Betty Lou recaps, there was no piano accompaniment to the hymns that past Sunday morning as Mother Cindy Lou's back was covered in axel grease to mend the sores that darn blasted cat needing put down put as is no normal cat but a demon from hell, and her owner too, Wendy Lou," as Mother Cindy Lou was in a ferocious mood and perhaps should be seeking peace in humble prayer in a quiet monastic place, her bedroom as Colville City was so small everyone spied on everyone else from boredom.

So, drawing the curtains is recommended.

There was a spacious cleared flooring at the front of the church where a camp bed had been set up and lying in it, Father Cindy Lou with a gunshot leg, self-inflicted as the man was a fool. A man who took orders from Mother Cindy Lou and not his black and white cow Texas Long Horn leather covered James Bible. It was obvious he was not a vegan as leather smells forever.

Church security was his job as he was warden, and a giant hole now existed where the church front door had been, until a police patrol vehicle took that out.

And the sad thing was the bill would go to the police department who would hand it over to the City Council who would up the rates and recoup.

The church goers would in the end pay for a new church door and that breezy roof hole where white stuff periodically rained through.

"You are sinners, this is The Lord's punishment upon you," the pastor seeing an opportunity to scare them to hell and then hand them the collection box.

Fear of The Almighty always made them generous.

This was a poor miserable church as he took his wages from the donations, he was needing a Revival Camp in Las Vergas for tired pastors, then a sailing holiday on a ship that doubled as a floating bible school as the ship circled Polynesia.

It would be a long revival vacation, the church was now open to elements and that meant Alaskan freezing cold, he did be back when his congregation had fixed the holes and hopefully put in central heating.

Pipes would run from the church to their houses, it would be their heat they did be giving, bless them.

Still Betty Lou recap

Then two shadows fell across Father Cindy Lou and the rest of the congregation.

"Sorry I am late," Medium Wendy Lou and sat at the back.

The other shadow stood still and waited till a hymn started then played mouth organ, and everyone sighed relief as thought he was taking a pistol from his lumber jacket to shoot them all dead; this was America.

"Well, those things happened," Betty Lou who like other spirits were aware of earthly frolics as where trapped themselves in spirit energy level three, like some supernatural lift, the same one Saint Paul visited on the way to Damascus. *"Yes, I remember seeing him chatting to angels learning the secrets of heaven that he kept to himself,"* so Betty Lou was fibbing about her age and being a contestant in the Colville Beauty Contest 1920. *"Listen, a girl never admits her age."*

ANYWAY, *"that is me blithering, just cannot stop when I start."*

"So shut up then," Joseph.

*"Ha giggle **snort** that I like,"* one of them angels.

Now the church might be full of heavenly kinetic energy, **but dark shadows were gathering on the outskirts of town.**

A tall dark strange man, him again, had a hand stuffed in a green trench coat front and on his head, an 1812 Black Cock Hat, a tri color ribbon was sewn onto the left side of the hat.

With great difficulty he managed a single lensed binocular.

He was spying and giving orders, he was away in a illusionary world.

A single headphone was plastered into his left ear, 1812 played, he needed cannon, he did not have any, so sounds of cannon was just as good, any cannon, as long as it went 'BOOM.'

A mobile phone hung from his neck, 'The Alamo' was playing with American heroes, and Mexican ones, them that were called extras.

"I do believe I am hallucinating Clay for I surely see critters from hell gathering on the ends of Main Street Clay," Sheriff Bottom fingering his pistols that were not present.

"Better get the Mounties, correction State troopers Nathan," Clay being familiar. The sheriff ignored the coziness of words as he felt both had journeyed to their 'LITTLE BIGHORNS' this day so familiarity was all right, they were going to heaven, by gone were by gone.

On each end of Main Street was a big hairy ape standing eight no nine feet from unshod BIG FEET to the red mass of curled matted hair on top the skull cap.

Behind this animal was a horde of red baboons. Well, they

must exist as they were here, but why?

And they was pure ugliness as those red bums was big and being just big monkeys started to act censored play whatever stuff, so Sheriff Nathan Bottom looked through them as if they did not exist, a silly thing to do as this lot needed watching, not for the monkey porn but 'WHO KNOWS WHAT WHERE THEY DID GO?'

And half of Colville ignored them as thought they were invasive immigrant lumber jacks, gold panners, lost tourists, paranormal hunters, elves, all come late to celebrate the 4th July, *"see they did not belong to the temperance societies, titter"*, the towns folk was half drunk, and the other half-drunk population thought they was poor relatives of The Native Americans living here.

"BANG," and was repeated till the jail house front door lock fell apart as Father Cindy Lou blasted the door lock.

"Mother Cindy Lou, I have been hit by splinters, I need a doctor," and was Father Cindy Lou who had stood to close while blasting away at the door lock.

"I am in," Mother Cindy Lou triumphantly and walked up to the sheriff and tossed a lynch necktie over his head.

And puffed away so choked the room out.

"Rattle," and was not Rattling Snake, there was a snake in here with my law boys, it was that cute baby and here it comes, a slithering out of a mouse hole, still skinny as the wise mice had left hearing 'rattle,' not like the brave fearless idiotic lawmen.
"Who in their right minds did stay in a room with a venomous rattler?"

"I hear a rattle snake," Clay Eagle studying the red baboons playing games.

"Strange you said that Clay, I hear a rattler too," the sheriff and both men intently listened for although Sunday, Colville City was bustling.

It was the 4th July, Independence day, Alaskans celebrate not victory over the British but from Tzarists Russia, for the United States bought Alaska from Russia, so we people from the far north see history slightly bent.

"Best not look down sheriff, that rattler is all around your feet, that knee high leather boots you got on sheriff, no need to worry them fangs will not penetrate those boots," Clay's advice.

"Best not move either young handsome man," a stranger's voice and Clay felt the coldness of steel against his throat. How did the strange man get in the jailhouse.
Was it because the lawmen were preoccupied with the rattler.
Or ogling too much at the dancing girls outside.
Or wondering when Mother Cindy Lou did become a sweet elderly kind lady?

"Do something Clay, I am just a spirit, if I kick spit and punch the stranger nothing happens, and those dark imps on his shoulders are nasty," Rattling Snake, Clay's guide.

Then Clay felt the razor slide down his back to his sitting parts and the stranger behind moaned, *"If I cannot have you, the snakes will and will make sure no one else does CLAY, I watched you sneak into Medium Wendy Lou's house by the back door at nights, you stop that as are my handsome boy now, understand,"* the excited male voice behind Clay whose hand held a cutthroat to Clay's sitting parts.

"Medium Wendy, you and her, really," the sheriff turning his head to look at Clay and saw a good bit of their attacker who realizing he had been seen went hay wire in the head.

"Sparks and smoke came from his ears and thunderbolts from his bum, giggle chuckle snigger."

I should never have worried; Mother Cindy Lou was here and a baby rattler.

The strange man stepped this way and that to slice Sheriff Bottom this way and that and stood on the cute baby rattler that earlier had slithered in, remember.

He also stood on Mother Cindy Lou's corns.

Mother Cindy Lou who did not realize that here was the murderer but being her had stood back some admiring the strange man's rippling back muscles that shone with the spray on wind and rain proof army plastic spray.

She also ogled his rump and almost fainted as that rump was stuffed into a toadstool print 8 sizes to small 'Y' Front, and how did she know, **it was her secret.**

Anyway, "Sh*t I am bit good," the strange, excited man and was stabbed many times by a knitting needle all good mothers keep for emergencies, along with spare socks, bras, knickers, Y fronts, and condoms, peanut butter and jam spread sandwiches.

"I am bit all over," the man not knowing the difference between a rattler bite and a knitting needle, but ran back to his pickup truck shaking the rattler off his knee-high BIG FOOT rubber boots, and inside found what he wanted, a handgun that he fired at our boys and vials of antivenom he injected himself with, then drove away screaming into his microphone so the **dark woods** vibrated to, and Colville City below, **"Clay Eagle you are my handsome boy, you hear me or Sylvia Lou here my cutthroat will visit your sitting places."**

And was unfortunate the man did not drive off the road down a thousand-foot ravine, where his pickup truck would burst into flames and from those flames, "I hate you Clay, you cheated on me with that BI**CH," and ended the story, saved lots of actors and extras dying in this ridiculous tale.

"You bit sheriff?" Clay asked as both men were safe from the rattling rattler.

"Did you know him Deputy Clay," Sheriff Bottom asked full of suspicion, "he knew you Deputy," making it formal, "DOES Wendy know you are on first names with that guy?" Bottom was being cruel as comes from finding out you wasted your time purchasing that diamond ring on Higher Purchase.

"No Sheriff, but how come you were all alone with him up in the **dark woods** when I came to rescue you?" Clay not going to show Wendy the diamond ring he bought with two months' salary as had survived on cooking lessons with Wendy Lou, and what takeaways drunks just dropped.

"Chicken Fajita.
Gobbler pancakes.
Pumpkin and chocolate mash.
Sweet corn and refried beans Texas style," song by unseen nighttime animals who had watched him singing for you.

And Father Cindy Lou although desperately needing a doctor did not take kindly to being lifted and thrown out of the strange man's way running to his pickup.

So shot at him and blew the strange mans right big toe off.

If that baby rattler that the strange man had not shaken off himself had not landed on Father Cindy Lou, the aim would have been better and the story ended.

"Oh, Sweet Jesus a rattler just but me," Father Cindy Lou afraid he was going to the other place below for sneaking into Little Joes nightly.

"Are you his guardian angel, I see church goers get an angel and the common folks, the likes of me and Joseph, well you better tell him that being a baby rattler used up its venom biting the strange man, Father Cindy Lou is going to give himself a cardiac arrest, giggle."

"Out of my way," and was Mother Cindy Lou who picked up her man's gun and blasted away at the retreating pick up.

"Oh God forgive me, I will stay and serve my flock," the pastor ahead clutching his stomach sticking a finger in a bullet hole to plug it.

"My left ear just vanished, what idiot is shooting at me," **the strange man** doing a terrific job at losing body parts, and just did not know when to stop.

And she put a hole through Sheriff Bottoms' ten-gallon hat.

"Just got to wear this one as has run out of spares, besides the bullet hole adds class Clay."

"Sure, does Sheriff," and Clay stuck a finger in the hole making it a huge hole, and "lucky for him Nathan Bottom was wearing the hat so did not notice, *"giggle."*

Anyway,

"Clay Eagle you are my handsome boy, you hear me or Sylvia Lou here my cutthroat will visit your sitting places."

"The whole town heard the strange man's accusing voice as it drifted down to the Sunday good people who are looking up this way Clay," Rattling Snake his guide the accusingly foolish familiar as should know his human as hangs about him 24/24 or should except when the human is in the privy or with Medium Wendy Lou watching latest drive-in movies from her back bedroom window, **notice not parlor window,** so should know he has nothing to do with the strange man *"and would like to handcuff him, places, giggle a naught Betty Lou joke."*

"And we know where to stuff them jokes," Fili Pek sour Betty Lou did not like him, but he had forgotten and she admired him going all alone to confront the bad dark imps to save her Clay, and of course her charge, the shrimp under the ten-gallon hat, but that was her privilege to keep **that secret.**

"Always knew something queer about that boy," yes it was her, Mother Cindy Lou looking up so relaxed her hold on her husband while he waited for help to get into a wheelchair that miraculously a Little Joe regular had pushed his way, and to eat the Sunday Diner for Sunday Turkey Burger, pumpkin mash and fries and gallons of ketchup and a gallon of black coffee, *"and why the man never sleeps and wanders nighttime, giggle."*

Soon the burger bar did be filled with customers lounging outside enjoying the 4th July and celebrations to start. They were Alaskans and were not going to let little fairy tale legends frighten them away from the 4th July.

And the floats, chorus girls and cheer leaders somersaulted here and there over Little Joe's regulars now sitting outside on the wooden planked pavement while under those planks, rattlers, but was all right, they had retreated away from the mayhem as had been up nighttime rodent catching.

" **Colville City was a clean city.**
   The trash cans were emptied by hungry drunks.
   Red baboons and Big Foot.
   Licked the trash cans sparkling clean.
   So, scarps left for the rodents,
   and most of these poor defenseless rats
   kept the rattlers fat and content.
   So left you alone." A rattler song on the wind sang by ghost pioneer folks.

And a Little Joe regular was seen crawling to the bar moaning, "someone pinched my wheelchair."

Anyway, Betty Lou recap time.
"Gawd woman my kingdom for an ambulance," Father Cindy Lou seeing his future as without his wife's hold on him he slithered down onto the road and rolled into the middle, just as Little Joe's dancers danced all over him.

He should have been in the **Male 10th Kingdom of Bliss,** all them perfumed trainers about him, ogling shaved legs and staring at belly buttons?

"Hi ya Father Cindy Lou," they shouted and blew kisses at him and Mother and Granny Cindy Lou noticed, so did Grandad Cindy Lou, twenty cousins and ten ancestry hunters descended from them.

"Lucky bas****," they whispered making sure their woman folk did not hear, but them women folk knew how to read their lips, so they was dead meat later.

He should have been in the **Male 10th Kingdom of Bliss** but was not as those trainers kicked his eyeballs, stuck in his ears, and went up his bum.

It was Male 10th Kingdom of HELL.

Then the High School cheer leaders did their totem pole with the girls one upon the other to the one at the top waving at folks, and Father Cindy Lou at the bottom unable to glance up at all them pretty ankles in white socks and elastic covered bums; he should have been in the Male 10th Kingdom of Bliss but as stated he was on the bottom, flattened, gasping for breath, going blue and saw the red baboons and Big Feet at the ends of Main Steet, but could not warm anyone as a cheer leader trainer was in his mouth.

It did not taste any different because it belonged to a pretty ankle, it tasted just like all the other soles in Colville City, of dust, dog dung, cat pee and drunk illness.

It was Male 10th Kingdom of Hell.

Besides no one did believe him about the monsters, he was that crank Father Cindy Lou who spent every night in Little Joes and not the wife's, and knowing Mother Cindy Lou, towns folk had sympathy for him and if he went garbling, "garbling as a trainer was struggling to free itself from his mouth, that monsters were in town, he did lose all that empathy, understanding, sympathy, compassion and walk the other side of the street and, "Junior stay away from Nuttery Father Cindy Lou," and throw a well-aimed plastic dinosaur at the back of his head.

He remained silent and waited for the trainer to vacate his mouth so he did be free to enjoy the rest of the floats and their dancing girls.

"He deserved everything that was to roll over him rutting him

good, snigger."

Then the High School Float passed over him and the yellow school bus stopped and the girls and boys dressed as 'Tramps and Tarts' inside waving at the windows stopped waving.

"Yeh, that is the idea, take a breath and then push the school bus wheel off your crotch Father Cindy Lou," and hid my titter as he deserved it the ogling boggler.

"You are so cruel Betty Lou," Joseph glad he was dead and not under that heavy bus.

"Honey, I am not cruel to you am I?" I had been influenced by Joseph's earlier act of bravery. And Joseph did not call mea bad name, *'honey'*, get them every time.

Anyway, no one noticed, the floats stopped, everyone was staring up at Clay Eagle and Sheriff Bottom with suspicious Sunday eyes, waiting for the men to well if they was a man and women, smooch, and prove everyone correct, there was something funny about their lawmen.

"They had gone to the jailhouse roof to watch where the 4x4 stranger's pick up went to up the road out of Colville and get a rough idea where the strange man lived, then go shot him up with a tranquilizer gun as Clay was out of bullets for his Colt six shooters.

When would Amazon Prime deliver those bazookas.

He had clicked special delivery so where were those weapons.

He had also ticked a hundred shells and used the sheriff Bottom's credit card lying on the jailhouse desk.

He knew Bottom did get a refund from the councilors, it was a sheriff benefit, weapons, whereas poor deputies just got their washing and cooking done for them by Wendy Lou's.

Now they had done so much aerial sailing these days had become afraid of heights, so the lawmen were hugging each other on the edge of the jail house roof, afraid they did fall over.

"If I fall so is he and Wendy will have none of us," Sheriff Bottom.

"If I fall he is coming to and Wendy can mourn," Clay Eagle and being a spirit read their murderous lawmen thoughts, and shamed.

Would my Joseph think like that, and was ill over *"my,"* I needed to wake up from eternal sleep.

So, explains why everything in Colville had stopped, they were watching them, all except father Cindy Lou who was about dead under that yellow school bus.

"Are they going to kiss," just takes one of Little Joe's customers.

*

It was a real Sunday gathering full of angels and spirit people.

A short prayer to 'Creator Spirit' and thanks and a call for guidance in dealing with these stubborn folks.
And was rich as we were guides.

"They will never live it down Joseph," the Boss Angel.

"Mum mummy," Joseph as we all understood all was his fault.

"Never mind Joseph," Boss Angel, you know it was the way he said 'Joseph' you felt sorry for the ghost.

"*They were your responsibility Joseph,*" Boss again and I noticed we had all silently moved away from Joseph.

"*Look Josephine,*" the minor other angel to be annoying and opened a portal in our heaven, "*did I forget to mention we were on Saint Paul's Level Three Light Level, well we were, so this turbulent portal opens from which groans, gnashing of teeth, 'stinky Windies,' calls for water and deliver letters to living loved ones to warn them against living it up on the solid energy plane called Planet Earth,*" and so Betty Lou rested after that long winded speech.

Joseph's hair was blown off as wind came out the portal, well, he wore a wig, that came with him to the After Life, he was bald.

Then the white smock he was wearing same time was torn away from his body to reveal interesting sitting parts and ugly knees but the minor angel Number Two sensing my anticipation closed the portal.

"*Well Joseph?*" Boss Angel.
"*I will embrace their weaknesses as my own and hey wait a moment, I am Sheriff Nathan Bottom's guide, not Clay's, where is that snake?*"

"*Rattling Snake if you do not mind, do you mind helping out Josephine.*"

He lost it, poor Joseph, being put down by angels was one thing, buy by a snake quite another.

It took a frizzle and zapping of Light sent from a trident Boss Angel held that no one noticed, to levitate Joseph away and drop him three levels back to Earth.

"*Help,*" Joseph screamed and was a long scream that seemed

to last an eternity but was over in a puff.

"Rattling Snake, you must rattle louder, ha snort giggle," Boss Angel who loved his comedy.

"I salute your wisdom Great One," Rattling Snake doing some sickening slithering.

"Oh, I forgot, I promised Joseph he could wave to his sweet mother, be a dead Betty Lou and fetch him back."

"My angel commands and I obey, I hurry," for we girls know the weakness of men, and this Boss Angel was a male, maybe a Nephilim, a bad angel that sired giants with Earth girls because like me, they were all sweet Betty Lou's, who get away with cheek as we own shaved legs.

And behind me I felt angelic eyes burning my transparent rump, so tittered, jumped and twirled and fell through the portal and turned into a white dove.

"Boss Angel, she is no better than Joseph, she has got to go," the second angel sealing his own removal.

And there was Joseph tugging at Sheriff Bottom and used so much spirit energy tugged Bottom away off the roof, so a sudden wind gust blew him down the road hanging onto his cowboy hat, over the celebrations and towards the **dark woods** para gliding without a license.

It was some wind.

Why he wanted a cowboy hat in Alaska Gawd Knows, a beaver hat, wolf shaman skin hat, an Native American Chief headdress, or a baseball cap with Eat at Mine than what he wore and the wind wanted and the wind got.

Clay listening to me ran to the patrol car and put on a spare zip up jacket, this was not California and drove after his sheriff hanging onto his hat, now about five hundred feet in the Alaskan sky.

"Ooh," from the watching crowd and "Think the gay lawman will fall?" Granddad Cindy Lou and Granny Cindy Lou took bets from the crowd, "Ooh."

"Hey, look his Native American boyfriend is driving after him," Mother Cindy Lou and "five to one the sheriff drops before Clay gets to him," from an unknown in the crowd and would become known if won.

And Clay smelt something bad in the air, it was drifting up from Colville City and next to us.

How does a spirit ghost smell, **no idea**, we see you to in the shower, **no idea**, we see you on the privy, **no idea**, we see you at Joes ogling the waitresses and trying to get one home, we see you open the wallet next day and gasp in terror over a missing credit card, we see, **no idea** how.

And the badness beside us was residual energy left by that Tall Dark Stranger covered in band aid and now slumped over his steering wheel from an overdose of anti-venom, and yes he drove his expensive 4 by 4 off the road as it was designed to do so, but not the way the stranger drove it off, straight off through a crash barrier so it froze momentarily, giving the idiot gripping the wheel time to shout, "I hate you Clay," and as the 4 by 4 dropped he added, "I lied Clay, I love you Johnny too, I love Clay more, no I love Bald Pete who lies a moldering in the grave ha snort ha titter giggle," and passed out mercifully as the car landed on a slope and down it went a half mile to the gravel beach of Colville River.

He was a bad man and deserved the water lapping through the doors to soak his feet.

The water was cold, so maybe the stranger did die of hyperthermia and save the law finding him, but wait a moment, they needed him if he was fast becoming a suspect murderer, Sheriff, Clay, he was yes no a suspect?

"Wake up useless human," his dark imps panicking they were about to be out of a job and heard from a portal of Light, "Not his Time," and just like that the stranger woke up, allowed his head to spin, then because he knew he had an expensive 4 by 4 drove through the shallows till he reached 'Colville City Picnic Park, no Littering of Trash, DO NOT FEEED THE GRISSLIES,' sign, turned into it leaving tire marks managed to drive into the mobile toilets so they were no more, knocked over and crushed ten picnic tables, entangled the netball net, knocked down the basket ball posts, drove into the seating area for sport fans and vanished.

Colville City Picnic Park did not exist.

This stranger did not like picnic areas, perhaps a nasty childhood memory and the dark imps were elated, so were the black bears and one grisly who had no need to fight over the squashed trash cans full of fly blown human left-over picnic food, tasty Southern Louisiana fried chicken, some Colonel chicken thighs, chili laced hot dogs the bears liked as gave them the 'oh la, la' tummy feeling.

And lots of indigestible rubbish, plastic cups as wanted the coffee and sugar at the bottom.

And lots of used protectives as did not know what they was eating but when they WINDED blew foot long balloons from the other end, as the picnic area was a lovers paradise, not quite in the **dark woods** full of red baboons and Big Foot, and at the same time with a clear road straight back to town at 80 m.p.h. if any Alaskan Triangle Monsters showed up, especially during

Halloween.

But this strange man was not my concern, Joseph so thinking of him found him.

Joseph was guiding the ten-gallon hat to land in front of the speeding approaching deputy car Clay drove at 120 m.p.h.

"What are you thinking of Joseph," I asked and *"I am aiming for the open window."*

And all Colville City below remembered the hit film about two gay person cowboys, "And now we got ourselves two gay person lawmen," Mother Cindy Lou and spat Tobacco and "meow."

As much as she shook her right leg that cat clung on, so she grabbed it by the tail, swung it, and it landed on top of 'Exotic Alaskan takeaway Pizza float,' and the left claws unclipped a bra on a well, looked like a peperoni or garlic four cheese slice and the girl clutching her front fell, slid down the front and got stuck on the olive.

"Wow," "Oh," "Encore," from the spell bound townsfolk.

"They say elephants never forget, either do cats, and this one had the whole Cindy Lou kin to talon, except for Granny Cindy Lou who carried salmon treats.
And the kin ran in front of floats that hit the brakes, so always pretty ankles in skimpy thermal floozy wear, flew off the floats into the arms of 'KIN' DRUNKS in the crowds.

"Help mum," was heard often and mum in Colville City you did not tinker with.

"Give me back my daughter you pervert," a mother as

the drunk disappeared into Little Joes, and there were many drunks flowing inro LITTLE JOES with float jet sum, so became overcrowded and hot, so little Joe blasted a shot gun to clear them out, into the frying pans, butchering implements, guns, arrows, fishing nets and tins of spray paint of the mothers.

It was a one-way battle for what drunk can stand for long before he see or she sees double, so was massacred.

"Mummy I love you," a daughter.

"Let us go get a gobbler burger and banana chocolate brownie fudge," and did.

"Mummy," the drunks and mummy in heaven was ashamed and did not come, but lots of **dark imps** did, drunk also for they was **dark imps** of course.

And one mangy cat was responsible.

CHAPTER 5 THE 4TH JULY FLOATS

He was not lucky Main Street was Short Street.

Yes, the 4th July was here and Turkey Burgers Galore, and baby milk with a tint of sage and onion.

What happened to the para glide

At four hundred feet Sheriff Bottom let go and fell to Earth.

"It came out of the sky,
The Thunder Bird,
Vroom and whir,
The Mighty Thunder Bird came to eat him.
Thunder Birds are not budgies.
And the falling sheriff collided with it.
Ten feet from the ground he fell off.
What was The Thunder Bird?

'Amazon,' was stamped on the drones wings." Real birds admiring the drones flight, and never lost the cargo, never mind Bottom, he did not count as a valuable order.

And the deputy vehicle was a mess, rips, and dents from sailing off roads, and was lucky for Sheriff Bottom it was.

"I am coming friend, I am sorry we fell out, I will save you friend," Clay Eagle anxious he could not save his friend.

And through the rip in the car roof Bottom arrived.

"Tonka Almighty," Clay exclaimed and lost control of the vehicle.

"Look they are sailing again," an onlooker next to Mother Cindy Lou who smirked, she was going to get her necktie party after all.

SO, "Clay where you been sitting?" Sheriff Bottom asked staring at his deputy's sitting bit upside down as his feet stuck out the car roof.

"Sheriff, I thought you and Cindy Lou were regular baking partners Wednesday night offs?" Clay reminding his ex-friend he was straight and now a little worried and should be, he was hearing Granny Cindy Lou's rattling noises about gay lawmen.

"Your bum Clay," Nathan hollered and although these men had been working together since Mountain Men Times, people change, look at all the thousands of unsolved disappearances in the Alaskan Triangle, the air was infested with other worldly news that made your thinking wonky.

Nathan reached out to grab Clay's bum so even I was aghast, and Snake Rattler rattled incessantly so became a pest.

*"Was Mother Cindy Lou correct about Sheriff Bottom, was he a gay Sheriff Bottom, and **was a secret** I did not even know, was he?"*

And Clay jumped afraid Nathan was a secret gay person, and after all these years and yes, explains the teddy print 'Y' Fronts, the pile of condoms always in the sheriff's glove compartment, and his long drives out of town, where did he go, to a secretive gay meeting?

And Nathan jumped with these words, "Keep jumping there is a rattler at on your bum Clay," and I looked and yes I was so embarrassed blaming Clay's guide for that rattling ear piercing sound and thinking gay of Bottom, *"Aw it was just that baby again just out of its skin,"* I whispered to Nathan who clutched his ears while he jumped higher, but it was what he took off Clay's sitting bit that was interesting.

A big toe shot off someone's foot as D.N.A. evidence and mouth organ music was played.

'High Noon,' drifting from the **dark woods** to us, we were being watched. The boys did never live this behavior down.

"Clay come back here," Nathan watching his deputy jump and leap full of refried beans towards Colville City and the floats.

A baby rattler was jumping and leaping with him, thinking Clay was mummy perhaps or just being a mean rattler that fancied biting Clay.

And the patrol car glided down as the air currents flowing through the rips and dents made it a metal junkyard of a parachute and landed quietly for once on Main Street and Bottom fell out as was moving about to get a better view of Clay, and never noticed a hole in the car floor.

"There better be a turkey burger left for me," Nathan Bottom grumped wiping Main Street off him, and went for the patrol car and a few feet from the vehicle dropped a right hand to his colt in his make belief holster, that he never wore as a vet had given him tranquilizers and weapons to fire them, in the vehicle where a shadow sat in the passenger seat, where and who was it, **and was a secret**.

A SHADOWY FIGURE it was.

"How did he get in a police vehicle that is self-locking against parked theft and **was a secret?**" Nathan asked himself peering at the human inside as he gingerly ducked about his patrol vehicle trying to see who was in his patrol vehicle.

"The problem was that the shrimp was so small he was jumping up and down to look over the vehicle window.

"What is that creep doing behind that vehicle," Granny Cindy Lou always on the look for the DISGUST.

"Clay was right, get the Mounties sheriff," I spoke to an ear.

Nathan swatted the ear and knocked himself out.

"Oh, Joseph come here," and vanished leaving Joseph to get blamed.

'Sweet Alabama' filled our ears, we can hear to but easier to say what I did.

"Gawd she do not half blither when started," Joseph seeing an opportunity to get one in at the FEMALE KIND.

And the engine started up and the patrol vehicle drove down Main Street passing Clay jumping about avoiding that one 'pissed off' baby rattler.

"Sheriff forgive me," Clay shouted at the passing patrol car and as it did not stop, "I thought we were friends," "*tell him you will tell your sister he was seeing Cindy Lou,*" a dark imp seeing an opportunity to be opportunists took the chance to be opportunist and give DARK UNFORGIVING ADVICE.

And in a flash of moonshine Snake Rattle appeared to fight the Dark Imp.

A faint mouth organ could be heard 'Johnny Come Home' then the sound of a police siren to clear the crowds as an empty police patrol vehicle stuck in first slowly moved into the gaiety of Font Activities.

""Sh*t," there is a drunk sheriff behind the wheel," a someone shouted who did not vote for Nathan to be sheriff.

"Nope, it is that Native American, knew we could not trust him," a Yupik Indian that Europeans called Eskimos who wanted the deputy job, but because he hunted in a kayak most of the time, hardly anyone knew he existed, except for a strange man who bought his illegal skins hunted in his kayak made of skins, so was an illegal boat needing impounding.

*"And have this Yupik handed over to Clay for interrogation, Athabaskan Indian style, **would Clay** string him up over a blazing fire sweating information from the Yupik, **would Clay** pull the Yupik's teeth out with a pimple tweezer, did Clay give up and leave the Yupik in a cell with these words, "we turn the heating off at night in the jail house as Colville City has no need of a goal."* Joseph hoping for a quick end to this Sheriff Nathan Bottom tale so he could be given the job of guide to a circus clown, *"as Joseph saw one in a circus as a boy and has this thing about clown dolls and circus fire breathing dragons, Joseph is deranged and not fit to be a guide giggle, guess who?"*

And the float parade ended because of a patrol car stuck in first and as the celebrations fell quiet, only the sizzling turkey burgers were heard and another sizzling sound, a Big Foot who had sneaked into town to raid the trash cans with other monsters was having a big leak.

And mouth organ music played a tune, 'Last Train to Yuma,' and folks grew nervous and looked about and screamed, there on the roof tops RED BABOONS who not as smart as those Big Feet critters were silhouetted and seen.

"Where is the sheriff, never here when you need him, glad I never voted for him," a disgruntled man unsteady on his feet as Joe's was open to alcoholic bottles, glass not plastic, so the citizens of Colville were proud they were not polluting The Last Great Wilderness, Alaska, but kept the local doctor and cottage hospital busy with cut feet, bottle fragments needing removed from thick skulls, inflamed liver treatments, and lonely modern Mountain Men, the loggers, the gold panners, them botanists, the cryptid hunters, fishermen. Tourists, abandoned delinquent children so the medical team was busy, and why some spirit guides suggested to the greedy doctor who owned the health Centre, dress his nurses up in French Maid Uniforms, so yes, $ floated out of the Cottage Hospital Roof, and loggers were suspected of taking an axe to a foot, gold panners swallowing a nugget needing panned from a sitting place, butterfly hunters chasing the French Maids about the small cramped cottage hospital with butterfly nets to nurses giggles, and joggers with sprained ankles peering, ogling, having their eye balls pop out from staring at frontage in revealing nurse outfits, yes $ drifted from the roof of the cottage hospital.

"And the thing is Colville was so remote was never told Alaska does not have sheriffs like the rest of the United States so was one reason these idiots never voted for a sheriff, they had State Troopers

and borrowed Mounties from neighboring British Columbia, so I ask you, how did they end up with Bottom and Clay?" Me, Joseph sh*t stirring to get out of this script, no sheriff no need for a guide, I did be free to roam the spirit realms doing what I wanted, being a hippy surfing the clouds.

"And what did cute little angry Joseph want?" I not hinting at a radio-controlled tank Santa forgot to give him, *"but angels with wings in short dresses as all artists paint angels as almost naked females, is that what you want JOSEPH?"* I calmy asked the other guide to Nathan Bottom.

"And where is Nathan Bottom?" A Boss Angel angry with Joseph for not being with his charge, but not me as I was wearing a short white skirt and low cleavage, yep I was going to get my wings before Joseph giggle titter as only pretty girl guides know how to titter giggle and reveal too much.

And it was all my fault as forgot to get Joseph back to wave at his mum, oh dear, I will call him 'honey' a few times and all will be forgiven, titter,

"Unruh," Boss Angel and vanished.

"I am onto you," the second lower angel so I showed a bit of shoulder.

"Cur," the angel, yep, works every time, time The Creator Spirit made angels out of females?

*

And Clay cleared the wooden pavements as he danced here and there to be away from a 'PISSED OFF BABY RATTLER.'

And out of town, the shadowy **figure driving the police vehicle stopped the car, opened a door, and pushed an unconscious sheriff out.**

He landed on his head wakening him where others it did have helped him remain unconscious, but the sheriff was different.

And a melody struck him, a chorus of Song Sparrows and varied Thrush birds gathered about him, squirrels and porcupines, a big black bear singing it's soul to him, and this is what they sang,

> **"Oh, Bottom listen to your guides,**
> **I am still here,**
> **Am I dead or alive,**
> **All I see is leaves and bones,**
> **All I smell is nappy stinks,**
> **And not from babies,**
> **All sheriff follow my melody,**
> **Am I dead or alive?"**

And the sheriff jumped a foot when he saw what he had held taken from Clay's sitting parts, a scalp, and the hair was red, so the victim was a redhead person that helped heaps.

Most folks here abouts had red hair from Scottish and Irish ancestors, so Nathan at arm's length checked the roots for red dye, and no, the red hair was genuine, so he sighed relief, it meant the victim was not of African descent, Native American, or other blonde blah whatever American tourist gone missing in the Alaskan Triangle, home to Red Baboons and Big Foot.

"Sheriff make sure you do not wipe your mouth after holding that," Joseph with good advice.

And the sheriff held it gingerly between his left fingers and followed the melody of rhythm and was easy to do as all them singing animals came with him.

And not once did the sheriff celebrate D.N.A. evidence was in his hand, why, he was a western old-fashioned sheriff that lived by the fast draw and was an imbecile that is why.

Then at first he put it down to imagination, but he was sure tall dark shadows were lurking in the woods, leaping from behind Alaskan Yellow Mountain Cedar to Alaskan Willow Tree branches to have them snap under the shadows weight, to fall amongst red, white spotted toadstools and vanish.

"Oh, sheriff where are your guns?" Joseph more worried about himself as those shadows had dark thingmabobs darker than imps wanting to know Joseph better.

"This sweet melody is a female, and if was a male, I ask myself, would I be stupid enough to venture this far from Colville, ALONE.

Where is my deputy?" Nathan asked so I asked Snake Rattle, *"Where is the man Clay, Baby Rattle, mummy want give you a cuddle?"* Oh, I was bad knowing I was protected by angels, especially Boss Angel.

> *"Call me Betty Lou,*
> **Fairest guide north of the Pesco,**
> **Prettiest guide west of Edmonton,**
>   *Bonniest guide west of the Pecos,*
>   *Voted best familiar east of the Baring Strait.*
>   *Soon to be given WINGS.*
>   *For only a girl GUIDE knows*
>   *Angels should be girls."*

And was ammunition for Joseph who finding Clay in an amorous statue position while Wendy Lou painted an oil on canvas of him feeding polar bears seals, forgot to tell him he was urgently needed, oh yes, he be a dead guide from Boss Angel when they met, but not to worry, Joseph was already dead.

A Betty Lou Recap

Little Bush People, Ircinrraaq or the homo floresiensis had come out of their borrows lifted into the breeze, carried by the breeze as so small and light to the edge of Colville City, and seeing mayhem due to a police patrol car stuck in first, ransacked every fridge in town, and as they left,

"Hey look, The Small Folk with my groceries," and only takes one.

"Yeh, lucky it is not the wolf folk, hey wait a minute it is still daylight," one of them.

"Never mind them, I see Big Foot sneaking out of Little Joes with a sack of pizza," another.

"Call the Mounties," another.
"Where is Sheriff Nathan Bottom," and was such an uproar the red baboons and all the monster cleared off to a more enlightened environment the **dark woods.**

"Go be a honey Clay and do your job out there," Medium Wendy Lou knackered from painting Clay on canvas riding a walrus holding a penguin in each hand.

And a shaved after shave smelling clean deputy walked down Main Street towards the jailhouse looking for his friend Sheriff Nathan Bottom who needed him urgently not be eaten all up by whatever was those shadows and was a shadow that had driven his patrol vehicle had dumped him on the road out of town.

Where they the same type of shadows? **It is a secret.**

And soulful mouth organ music filled the street of Main

Street, so even the red baboons stopped amongst the Alaskan Fir trees spell bound, locked in musical ecstasy, the foolish red baboons as Big Foot was coming your way and was partial to the red bottom found only on a red baboon of Alaska, the man eater of vanished joggers and tourists.

And a door opened to a wreck of a police patrol vehicle and Clay heard banjo music and a voice, **"Get in,"** and a puff of cigar smoke blinded him as he leaned in for a look, so was dragged in and found himself driving the car out of town.

Banjo, mouth organ and sing a long music came from the rear fender.

Clay wondered how he did that and the man and must be Johnny Christy.

The answer will be revealed shortly unless **it is a secret**.

*

"Jesus sweet Jesus," Clay having a cardiac arrest as seeing Nathan walking along the road, the car was filled with mouth organ music, so Clay having no police training in police patrol vehicles skidding on oily rainy roads, slipping following a truck of pigs, learning to swerve between bullets, computers thrown out of high-rise apartments, did what you and I did do if we was driving believing we were the sole occupants in that police patrol vehicle, nothing.

"Jailhouse Rock," Clay recognized the tune as the police patrol vehicle sped off the road into the **dark woods.**

"I thought I heard a car behind me, nope, nothing there but them creepy shadows," Nathan reassuring himself he was fine, nothing to fear from Clay's Native American Monster tales or late-night films watched with Cindy Lou, 'Were-wolf in Anchorage, Alaska,' "Frankenstein lives in frozen Alaska," "The

Owl Man of Colville City," and such tripe, *"and all he did have to do is acknowledge I exist, Betty Lou, much prettier than Cindy Lou and even more experienced as am MIND, giggle."*

*

"My Boss was looking at me funny as if I was about to be sent to Angel Academy and relieved of active duty," Boss Angel.

"Oh, goody gum drops about time, I see promotion for me coming," number two angel hiding, eves dropping in the angel realm wings, ha angel realm perimeter.

*

"Sweet Jesus," Clay as his patrol vehicle headed into a giant Alaskan cedar with a twenty-foot base, but a rut in the forest track swerved the car right **and towards Nathan** whom Clay saw, and saw shadows so was afraid as Native American Superstition rose in him.

"The Sdonalyasna Clay, do something," Snake Rattle being a helpful guide.

And the back door opened, and someone jumped out and the mouth organ music stopped.

And Clay should not have tried to look in his mirrors to see what had left his police patrol vehicle.

And Clay sort of half stretched half leaned over the back to grab that swinging open police car door of the patrol vehicle.

"And I rattled so much got hoarse, then shut my eyes so did not have to look and flicked on the police patrol vehicle siren to be helpful to both lawmen," Snake Rattler.

"Gawd where the flip are my guides?" Nathan turning his head to see where the police siren was coming from, admitting he had guides to help him, *"if he was nice to them, titter."*

"I am hear lover," me giving Nathan a wave from an orb of light, and he saw me as looked and not at the police patrol vehicle leaping out of the underbrush onto him.

Well, that is what he gets for ogling, titter, and where is he anyway, the police vehicle has bounced back onto the road and Nathan should be prone where I saw him last, with me greeting him in Spirit, lucky Nathan, but he was gone.

"Oh, Joseph you are needed honey, come here," no please as 'honey' used as to pass the blame onto him again, and be believed as Boss Angel favored me not Joseph who had ugly hairy nobly knees.

And there was Sheriff Nathan flattened against the passenger door, *"he had learned a trick or two from Johnny Christy."*

"Pull me in "Thai Boy," Nathan thinking Wendy Lou as Joseph was in his head *"yelling him to grab this, then throw Clay out, get in the driving seat, get the brakes on, no there are Sdonalyasna about, get the car straight, I do not want to die, hey I am dead, it is you who is going to die ha, ha laugh,"* Joseph seeing the humanoid bird like creatures in the shadows with two-foot-long beaks to peck you good till nothing left to peck, and they had a monkey tail.

And was all the fault of them first pet shop owners not locking the animal cages but left them open as they stopped selling pets and went gold panning as this was Alaska, and guess what bored animals get up to in the **dark lonely woods**, breed into Sdonalyasna, red baboons, little people, and Big Foot types, so we know who to blame and those Native Americans seeing them spread it far and wide to stop the settlers arriving and failed, gold was here.

Maybe we should look at the Native Americans a bit closer, are their villages flying The Star and Stripes, do they have local militia dressed in Pacific Japanese Imperial Army Uniforms to show their loyalty to The Star and Stripes?

"But sheriff just hold on, and for such a small twerp what big biceps you have," me Betty Lou drooling over those muscles, thinking she was it for I know I was it and get away with murder.

And Nathan pulled an arm off Clay literally to pull himself aboard the patrol vehicle that was pointing and leaping and rearing upon the back wheels, so smoke, noise, and flames shot from them into the **dark woods** setting them on fire.

"Well done, so what now Betty Lou?" Joseph going to blame me.

"Nothing, look it is the Colville Fire Department come to help our lawmen," I giggled and clapped my hands and turned Nathan's neck so he could see and joy at his deliverance.

"I think you broke his neck Betty Lou," Joseph prodding Nathan who looked dead.

"What had I done in my eagerness to make a man happy," and covered my transparent frontage as modesty was required now.

"NO, they are going to the Colville Picnic Area for the 4th July celebration picnic, where they give a prize of a live gobbler to the first contestant to pan a gold nugget from the Colville River, a basket of frozen microwave gobbler burgers and buns to the quickest logger to take down the top of the highest fir tree, and show the trophy as proof, yes a beauty contestant as well as behind the red and white fire truck a horde of vehicles of past ages, as wages was poor these parts, full of everyone in Colville wanting to ogle and mess up the wilderness.

But because of the small fire started the firemen and hordes of contestants beat the flames out and sprayed water on the trees and bush to make sure no red sparks remained so not an acorn was roasted and those squirrels do like them roasted and is them that play with matches and burn down whole forests just to eat roasted acorns, believe me.

"What idiots are responsible?" The Fire Chief, but *"faster Clay, put the foot down,"* as the police patrol vehicle sped away in a dust cloud that choked the brave fire fighters and blinded them, so none recognized the number plate on the police patrol vehicle but did know that police patrol vehicle siren anywhere.

"I never voted him sheriff, come to think of it, where did Sheriff Nathan Bottom come from?" The Fire Chief scratching his bald head under his white fire cap with a big gold eagle on the crest.

And no one could remember.

"Maybe he is a Big Foot in disguise," an idiot and takes only one and soon a serious discussion arose from what Alaskan monster Sheriff Nathan Bottom came from?

"But I knew, ever hear of Granny McFeed, supplier of children's teaching aids and in 'small print, lawmen for the west and further away places.' And I stopped helping Nathan and wondered if it could be true, was Nathan like me, an entity, and what made Clay, his faithful Tonto Native American, were both here in disguise, could they remember their past lives, titter ?

It meant Clay was mine, forget Joseph who I only called 'honey' to get my way and better forget those biceps on that shrimp.

My charge, Bottom was alive and I rejoiced and hugged him and kissed him till he about ripped his ears off trying to be rid of my possession.

"I never get any of that?" Joseph.

CHAPTER 6 STRANGER IN THE WOODS

*Stranger in the **dark woods***

I saw him plain as I can investigate the sun, so am not able to describe the strange man covered in band aid covering cutthroat cuts and snake bites as the sun is bright.

How he was still standing I can only guess at his inner strength which would impress any girl snort, whoops sorry, a memory of a snort came through with the giggle titter **snort, again**?

A tall man with black hair because the blackness stood out in heavenly sunlight.

He could be an African American, do not think so, as his hair was swimming gel flattened back like Mr. Johnny Depp.

His upper torso was triangular from gym enthusiasm or steroids and think it was glistening sweat, but the glimmer might be body bronze fake suntan, but that moisture droplets followed his muscle shapes, daddy, not mummy I am getting the shivers of delight.

So never heard: *"Boss Angel, she has got to go."*

"I will visit her forth with," Boss Angel letting the side down.

And it was he who a mile down a dirt track Joseph had urged Nathan Bottom to drive down, this tall strange sweaty man in just baggy combat fatigues, held up by a tight leather belt with a long flapping end stood in the road.

"Flap," it went, and should not as there was no breeze, just an evil presence so it made the flap, flap.

In one hand the cutthroat razor and in the other a severed head missing his scalp, so the skin dragged down to the eyeballs that stared a cement look that said it all, "I am not in heaven."

And his big shinny red boots glinted from the evil presence as no sunlight filtered through the Alaskan Fir trees, bird pooh from a Downy Woodpecker managed to hit his scalp repeatedly as those birds was in a festive mood.

Annoying him.

"Bu**er this," the man exploded excitedly wiping his head to remove the white stains and added, "Sh**t that is my ear lying on the mountain track," and as blood squirted about he bent down to pick up his severed right ear and laughed, "never felt a thing" and added, "Argh," as a police patrol car driven by careless lawmen ran over him, well he went over them smearing the windscreen in red stuff, blood, then thumped off the boot.

"A Big Foot?" Both lawmen asked, and Clay stretched to get

his unloaded Colt as unlike Nathan, a Colt, Wendy Lou, Betty Lou, alcohol free beer and a warm fire to roast cold feet against was needed in these parts.

And unlike Clay, Nathan reached for the glove compartment to get his tranquilizer pistol and darts, for he knew to cuddle into Cindy Lou and Wendy Lou, alcohol free beer and pizza was all that was needed when under a warm electric blanket.

And so, our lawmen cracked heads, uttered bad filthy words unimaginative adults use and stuck **the police patrol vehicle into reverse.**

"Arg," and a bump was heard and felt as the strange man needing his severed ear stitched back on stood up, see he was strong, and the car stopped against a spruce tree knocking a red baboon above off, watching if a free meal was available.

It landed on the stranger and after an angry exchange ran off with a left eyebrow, it was hungry unfortunate thing.

Well, the lawmen thought it was a red baboon as it disappeared down the track and managed to eat that ear, so the strange man looked symmetrical, a perfect artists portrait, no ears and blinded by the eyebrow wound.

"You got your Colt friend," all amnesty between the lawmen forgotten.

"Yeh friend, you got your tranquilizer pistol and handcuffs handy friend," Clay as both men had put aside they shared the same interests in Colville City so were best 'friends' again.

And Clay drove the police patrol vehicle forward after the strange man leaving a dented bumper and number plate at the foot of a spruce tree.

Several pearly white teeth with gold taken from Baldy Panner Pete were used as fillings, gone from the strangers mouth now embedded in the fender.

And mouth organ music filled the woods, an uplifting funeral march for the boys under tin star badges.

A hot cigar butt span through the air and with excellent aim disappeared into the strangers open zipper bit.

Before you can count to ten censored fuzz burned and smoked and the toothless strange man jumped up and ran straight home, knocking himself out against a tree branch.

And with flames shooting out of that zipper he rolled face down into a small stream, and started to drown, whoopee, the murderer got his desserts.

No, a friendly Big Foot picked him up and carried him home, tree branches meant nothing to this monster.

It was her again, the girl friend he denied and knew when to catch him, when he messed up trying to kill the lawmen.

Then an Amazon Prime Drone landed in front of the vehicle and the boys stopped quick, to quick.

"Sweet Jesus I bashed my head on the glove compartment Clay."

"Sweet Tonka, I need a dentist Nathan as bashed my mouth into the steering wheel."

"Think I damaged my privates on the tight seat belt I was thrown into Clay."

"Think I neutered myself Nathan on the seat belt too, who designed them, a woman?"

Clay was happy, Wendy Lou did think Nathan ugly and show Clay attention woof.

Nathan was happy, Wendy Lou did see Clay as an ugly now and shine on him, woof.

Clay was happy, the seat belt had left Nathan useless and Wendy did love him to bits, woof.

Nathan was happy, the seat belt had done a better job than the vet on Clay, Wendy was all his now, woof.

"Oh, Betty Lou can I look at your pretty ankle, woof, oh dear you have not got any ankle just white mist, not woofing over you," Fili Pek being annoying.

"Then I will not call you dear."

There was a ghostly silence, then, *"sorry Betty I was not thinking."*

I win every time, and rolled up translucent hold ups, *"Who gave you permission to call me Betty?'*

And the boys were armed with bazookas and Colt bullets thanks to a drone, from Amazon.

"Go get your man now lads," and spaghetti western music filled the **dark woods.**

Then the flick of a match and fresh cigar smoke was smelt.

Who was Johnny Christy, a secret you know. And in his pocket teeth with gold filings, DNA evidence or a perk of the job playing a mouth, **it is a secret.**

*

*"Boss Angel why what a surprise you out and about in these damp **dark woods**, why you will catch your death of cold titter giggle*

snort, sh**t, there it is again," Betty Lou.

"And will get worse if you fail your teaching role here with Nathan, my Betty Lou," Boss Angel sliding quickly under Betty Lou's transparent charms, and behind him Number Two angel, not called in heavenly realms because of the reference to certain physical needs. Just that it was rubbed in on Level Three After Life Zone by miscreant ghosts, he was on probation just like us your favorite guides you need as breakfast accompaniments.

Number Two with a straight face but any second about to crack into devilish laughter at Betty Lou's uncomfortable situation, the horrid angel if there was one, and yes , he was here.

Just call out, *"Number Two, where art thou?"* Snort giggle how do I get rid of this oink?

"We told you, do your job snort grunt," Boss Angel for nothing is hid in the heavens especially if you are A BOSS ANGEL allowing the likes of Betty Lou to get away with GUIDE SLACKNESS because she has transparent ammunition up front to distract a Boss Angel doing its job, To Serve and Protect and guide intelligent created evolved life below their wings.

"Hiss rattle ha rattle I find this so amusing Betty Lou being scalped," Snake Rattle not being careful with words so was sent to Clay with loud harp music in his ears so he got the message, *"DO YOUR GUIDE JOB rattlesnake,"* the latter words hissed *as a reincarnation threat* if he failed to help Clay Eagle.

"I am off," Betty Lou sneaking away through Snake's open portal and Boss Angel could not help a last furlong peek at where her calf muscles should have been, but was a ghost see, so was transparent so saw Number Two Angel sneaking away also.

"It is only Joseph I am left with to advice how to be a good ghostly

guide," Boss Angel but was wrong, for Joseph still had wit for you carry who you are when you go over, and what part goes over?

Physicists says the tube connecting neurons full of your memories is the bit that survives so PROOF of an AFTER LIFE at last, nope they went and refuted that, the proof is in my existence.

And since Joseph was a witty fellow since his English American was rubbish back in the gold rush days, smiled and laughed at everything said to and about him, but did not later say "Yes," to everything as learned he was giving away his gold mine stakes.

So learned "No," with a smile also, but they still lynched him smiling but was not a true smile but a true grit facial expression of a hanging man wanting air to breath, but this rope got in his way, so he went over to the After Life wishing he had learned American English.

And Boss Angel covered his mouth as grunts, snorts and oinks escaped him so fell to his transparent knees which was a challenging thing to do as he had none, but his wings he had and they sagged as he prayed:

> *"Oh, Creator Spirit, from you I came and so*
> *Did that lot.*
> *Forgive me my God,*
> *I am only an angel,*
> *Descended from the Nephilim,*
> *Allow me not their fallen ways,*
> *Come save me my God,*
>
> > ***Snort grunt oink,"*** and trembled

and fled the same way as the others, confused, not understanding why his prayer was rejected went trembling, fearful he would be sent to THAT PLACE, DAS BOAT, an overcrowded hell full of stale breath and stench of sauerkraut, a place where there were no light bulbs on.

"Learn your lessons NUMBER ONE," Boss Angel heard as his white energy mass entered the **dark woods** about our 'fools and horses.'

And up-front melody of New Age Music wafted to the physical lawmen scent organs, clasping the inside of those nostrils with hooks, as a voice broke through the melodious tuneful soul-searching music, designed to make anyone feel guilty of nothing.

> *"I am not sure I am dead or alive*
> *But am sure fed up where I am,*
> *So why am I still here and you there?*
> *Because you are useless faggots,"* the voice in the melody turned angry, then added,
> *"Oh, did I frighten you sweet little birds and mountain lions?*
> *Oh, did I frighten you snakes of the wood,*
> *Oh, did I frighten you sixteen giant elks,*
> *Oh, did I frighten you Big Foot?"* The beautiful sing song voice and all the critters calmed down except for those human critters Nathan and Clay.

"I am not leaving this police patrol vehicle friend Nathan."

"Well, one of us must investigate that sweet melody of pitch Clay, and it is not me as I am locking the police patrol vehicle doors so all them critters are out there and we in here, correction, me in here and that friendship cr*p do not work, as deputy I order you to get out and follow that Disney Film 'Snow White' nasal passage sounds, Deputy Clay."

"F*^%+"!K you sheriff, I quit," Clay sitting there with his tin badge still on which meant he had not quit. And then the car was surrounded by red bottom baboons that stuck the red bits on the windows that smeared in red bottom stuff.

And the two lawmen hugged each other in terror: many red bottom baboons opened the mouth and showed flesh eating teeth up close.

So, the windows misted, and the boys got relief for they could not see those red bums but smelt them so began to swoon.

"Honey pies wake up, look it is Betty Lou," I screamed in their minds and showed frontage to waken any male and make Dolly P. jealous.

"Rattle," Snake Rattle outside for he had read monkeys were afraid of snakes so added, *"hiss,"* but he had read books on African wildlife and these red bottom baboons ate rattle snakes here abouts so 'hissed' him back.

"Fag this," Snake Rattle in the huffs.

"It always takes a man with 'True Grit,' Joseph appearing to the red bottom baboons. *"Go away naughty monkeys, go play in the trees making baby red bottom baboon babies,"* and the idea pleased the nasty man-eating rattle snake red bottom baboons and went to the trees to play monkey, well, red bottom baboon games.

"Quick boys, get out of here," me Betty Lou urged our **heroes and without thinking they obeyed leaping from the safety of the police patrol vehicle** and ran up the forest fire road following the retreating melody of a siren, what else could the voice of a female belong to out here in these **dark woods,** the idiots, I meant drive away.

"A psychopathic killer wanting to make moccasins out of them,

giggle but did not sort as he had sent the baboons away to play big boy and big girl baboon games so should have grown a twisted little pink tail for that achievement?"

BETTY LOU WAS JEALOUS and annoyed her transparent stuff being transparent did not need covered up and was getting her in trouble with Boss Angel.

"More buttons need opening and a garter shown," Betty Lou looking for a leg to put a garter on, and as for the buttons they being translucent gave the impression Betty had many pointed bits.

And as the terrified lawmen made their way deeper into the woods, memories of last Saturday nights film in the drive in, which the boys watched free from the back window of the jailhouse, that remember looked onto the drive-in movie shows.

"Alaskan Were-Wolf Ate Me," the B film was titled with 'Victor Dela Charming' in the lead woof barking role, and the second B back up movie, "Frankenstein Meets Big Foot," starring Abbot and Nun, so memories was fresh in their minds, so teeth chattered and Nathan fumbled with fear frozen fingers to load his tranquilizer gun, it was still back in the police patrol vehicle, and Clay loaded his Colt and never looked to see where he put the bullets, all onto the forest floor.

"And what was the point of the amazon delivery drone snort grunt?"

"Betty is a pig, piggy Betty," Fili Pek not being called dear retaliated.

"These boys really needed to acknowledge spirit helping guides, well one did, Nathan, actually they needed the physical help of State Troopers as were soon to be dead, like me, then we could play big

monkey games on the clouds grunt," Betty Lou never knows when to 'shut up.'

And a twig snapped, a big twig, maybe a branch and SNAPPED loudly so the lawmen jumped six feet forward into foliage and stared into a face.

And the face was gentle, inquisitive, kind and with eyes full of understanding for the humans.

All trollup as was Big Foot and the beast understood humans needed to leave Big Foot Land or else, and it was OR ELSE TIME.

With a shaky hand Nathan aimed and fired a nonexistent tranquilizer gun at the ape that stood sixteen feet easy and was covered in thick matted reddish fur that was caked places so there was an almighty sh*t smell, overpowering it was.

Clay looked at Nathan with understanding and fired his Colt into the air to frighten Big Foot away.

"CLICK," and "CLICK, CLICK, CLICK, CLICK and CLICK" went the empty chambers and Nathan looked at his deputy and said, "well done Clay."

And the player of mouth organ music knew silence was the better call at the moment, so silence, not a chirp from any songbirds, a stinker from a scurrying skunk, a deep leaping over your head doing droppings as it went, nope, nothing.

CHAPTER 7   A GLIMPSE OF HIM,

Dionysus God of wine

Yes the stranger looking at himself in a mirror seeing not his usual self but a stranger, well he lost his ears so now had a slim lined wind aerodynamically designed face. All the gusty stuff blown about now missed those two absent ears sticking out, the grass tufts, the twigs, the small branches, the bigger branches, and angry animals on those branches that once could lash out at them BIG EARS.

And since he was a TOUGH MAN stuffed himself into FIVE sizes too small 'Y' FRONTS, as was being sensible about the sized, leopard print, and chose not to wear a shirt, lumber jacket or Granny's hand down ear puffs, he was a TOUGH MAN who without his wig was a BALD TOUGH MAN, so the racoons and wolverines on those branches slid down his waterproof back, and he cheated by spraying on army wind breaker and rain proof plastic spray, which was no match to natures claws.

BUT HE WAS A TOUGH MAN WHO GRITTED HIS TEETH and when he got back home gave himself another tetanus jab.

And the dark stranger smiled, and his handsome face was borrowed from the Athenian Acropolis where a statue of Dionysus, god of wine head vanished, some tourist full of mischief malcontent had cut off the marble head with a silent D.I.Y. marble cutter bought locally at discount, and to add confusion to injury left a note, scribbled on the two inch chewing gun greasy wrapper "We British took it to add to the Elgin Marbles in the British Museum, come visit swinging London," yes all crammed on that two ich rectangular chewy gum paper.

Marvelous what a steady hand and good eyesight can achieve?

And we take you to the missing head in a log cabin pioneer model self-assembly model A. Lincoln.

He was the tourist full of mischief malcontent that had cut off the marble head, the blah about the British FOG for the Greek police.

The head been tarted up as used as a wig holder, now a blonde wig, and the stone lips wiped and smeared with colored tasty lipsticks, as the wearer liked to lick the raspberry or mango from his lips, and the stone eyes painted white with green pupils, and the forehead long and cheeks prominent, why it is an Anglo Germanic head, then he changed the wig to a red head and wonders of prehistory it is a Celtic head he is fashioning himself into today, no, he had put on a 'Michael Jacky' curly black wig so must like dancing, ha, I give you a Betty Lou observation, with all those rattler bites and hypodermic needles for anti-venom sticking out from his legs, he be lucky to 'SAMBA,' and: he with a hammer knocked off the missing valuable Dionysus statue heads ears, not one ear, but both and foamed at the mouth and was no longer a handsome man Betty Lou did like to accidently meet trekking in the **dark woods**, if I had a physical body, titter snort, of good grief, grunt.

And the **dark woods** were filled with the jilted love song of a female Big Foot. On their wedding day he had sneaked away and the tribe were discussing going for him or leaving it, as he fed them frozen chops down at his Abraham Lincoln Class A D.I.Y. self-assembly log cabin.

A neat thing to have as could take it down and drive to another lonely spot in another State, and stat all over again.

"He might not have his ears but he had his marbles snort titter oh no."

ANYWAY.

Have you looked in the mirror and seen a stranger?

If the answer is yes, then ask yourself are you HIM in the **dark woods** intending bodily grievous harm to our hero lawmen? Are you ill from looking at the same old face in that mirror, then you need AJAX EPSOM salts daily and a triple dose of SENA laxatives at night, and Mr. SPARKLE tooth whitener, and a jar of Elvis Who? Hair Brill cream? And when you look at your face in the mirror again you will be happy and need a new mirror as smashed the old ones to bits taking your stress out on it, but all that salts, laxatives, toothy powder and hair tea leaf for lice did work and was worth every penny, cent, shekel, money you stole.

"Argh, my head is full of voices," **this strange man** clutching where his ears used to be so grabbed handfuls of his curly purple red dyed hair and pulled and tugged and the whole lot of dyed bush came away in his hands, and he was bald as a watermelon, and worse he gritted his teeth and showed Dracula filed teeth for biting folk and gaps were teeth he left on a fender.

And because his blood pressure went up his green-eyed contacts pinned out and he had small blood shot eyes, bad from lack of sleep, running about the **dark woods** and where else a strange man goes, perhaps to outhouses as not all log cabins have a septic tank you know, so are dug way down the back for the 'phew' is awful, titter grunt snort giggle, Gawd I am sorry, I will try and be a good guide, forgive me, please.

"Well down Betty Lou, your are glowing already and so am I," Boss Angel appearing beside my orb in the strangers log cabin, and the strange man's dark imps on his shoulders went wild and got him to scratch his bald head so red lines appeared and he screamed for he needed to cut his fingernails that were sharp and long, as he kept them that way for strange mysterious ways only a strange man who wondered *dark woods* looking for 'Red Riding Hood' did have.

He howled often and ran with Alaska's shapeshifters, half men half fish, so might really be suffering from lycanthropy illness, were-wolf imagination disease or be a real one, "HOWL titter," the grunt had gone as had done good.

"In fact, he no longer was what Betty Lou did accidently hope to bump into, in a dark secluded empty bird watchers hut as he was 'BLOOMING VILE LOOKING, ugly in other words."

And something else, the wig he took off he dumped in a spittoon full of tea tree oil, *"Yucky,"* so the strange man heard me and breezily tried to catch my orb, *"Which means he can see us, why are you here anyway girl, are you not supposed to be with your lawman oink grunt?"* Boss Angel worried his Boss above would not rid him of that wiggly tail hidden by his magnificent angelic shiny wings, *"and no wonder we can be seen,"* me just pushing the game blame onto my Boss.

And Boss Angel took me outside, how, used his energy that glowed more than my orb, in other words he overpowered me, just like a no-good man, but we were outside the pioneer self-assembly cabin.

I closed my eyes waiting for the kiss.

"You do not hear the music Boss Angel?" A big Boss Angel.

It was obvious this angel was going to be sacked as was looking at my frontage but because I had asked for forgiveness was covered with flying hummingbirds of all colors, maybe that was what my Boss was looking at, I did like to believe so.

"The music Boss, the melody, is fading, my are those hummingbirds on your melons, I mean," and Number Two Angel ran screaming for forgiveness into The Ether.

I looked down at my hummingbirds, *"It says all have a name, wonder which one is Mary Lou and Sarah Lou whoever they are?"*

"That one must be Sarah Lou grunt," Boss Angel not seeing the differences in prayer between the three of us.

And a phoenix all gold and shiny was seen to rise from my frontage, blinding Boss Angel, so made my escape following the sweet melody and waited down the track for Nathan Bottom.

A joyous feeling overcame me from that phoenix bird as it showered me in gold and knew I was not worthy of the help to change, I was me, Betty Lou, hapless guide North of Pecos, and saddened and waited silently.

While from the self-assembly log pioneer cabin a man screamed The Walls of Jericho down, The House of The Three Pigs down, London Bridge down and all the cute animals here abouts cleared out further for they had already moved from his evil presence.

For they had seen like me a **glimpse of the stranger.**

*

And the Gigantopithecus was not out to catch the two lawmen, yet, but to hurry them along.

The monster did it by staying upwind so the smell of pooh stuck to all that long hair was carried to the lawmen who gasped for air.

Now and again the ape threw rocks and beat trees with a rock.
It missed deliberately.

"Sheriff we are being stalked," Clay Eagle not looking anywhere but straight ahead quickening his steps hoping to reach the safety of the melodious singing that was becoming boring under the circumstances.
Now the sheriff being a tiny squirt was tiring as he had to take three steps for each of the magnificent specimen Clay Eagle took for each step, grunt, ah, snort, it is back, curse my womanish behavior.

"Child, I was a man one hundred percent and liked to look at women or why where they created, to have babies of course so no denying your womanish, just keep it under control some," and the voice was not manly or femslash but just an impression I had been spoken, so understood, and was about to rip away all the covering buttons on my translucent frontage when saw Angel Number Two approaching, and understood, a time and a place to be 'womanish' and the time now was calling for modesty or

Number Two might get the wrong impressions and think I was flirting with him.

Poor Number Two, and my sympathy for the angel vanished as imagining whatever an angel was, they had wings so must have chicken feet and what are the hands, were their chests covered in feathers and not hair, and what about those hanging bits, were they a birds, so was violently ill and the illness was a memory of what illness was in the physical realm. Somehow I escaped not being sent to The Outer Darkness immediately.

"Phew girl what you been eating," Number Two also remembering the smell of physical illness, so what had this NUMBER TWO been before, OF COURSE A NUMBER ONE, and tittered and did not snort.

Dumfounded I wondered why and thought about what the words given me about womanish ways, I was me, an idiot and made that way just like there are many colors of roses and birds, so hugged Number Two, so was ill again, on him.

"While that tart fancies herself I am warning my charge, Sheriff Bottom that he is in great danger and must hurry from this evil place," Joseph and the result was Sheriff Nathan clutched his head moaning.

"Them guides again Sheriff, what they say?" Clay his deputy navy blue shirt torn to bits from low tree branches to show Tarzan muscle, grunt, grunt, grunt titter, *"oh I am sorry."*

"My guide who earlier said he was Polish," Sheriff Bottom missing all the low branches as he walked under them, but that did not mean he was not suffering, he was stained in perspiration from taking more steps than Deputy Magnificent Clay, Argh oink giggle, *"Sheriff start running to the source of the repeated melody that I can sing backwards from hearing so often, you can too, oh poor man, just start running quick."*

"See was easy helping and asking forgiveness woman." It was the Ether itself talking to me and was comforting but myself and the other guides were not a comfort to the lawmen.

"What did your guides tell you sheriff?" Clay eager to know as he was all into 'Happy Hunting Ground After Life' legends.

"That we are going to die."

"F**k your guides, I am an Native American and got my own guide, oh Snake Rattle where art thou," Clay sweetly as the two entered a clearing.

"Rattle hiss," Snake Rattle avoiding responsibilities.

Tell him, that rattlesnake says same as I did, YOU ARE GOING TO DIE if you do not hurry, and do not look behind all right, which was good advice as that maniac covered in band aids and no longer anti venom syringes as they had fallen off, was 'a Cho echoing' round the bend hoot, hoot,' myself trying hard to keep human hope up but failed as my train impression was gibberish.

"Sweet Jesus I am never doubting I am a psychic and schizophrenic," the sheriff and ran faster than 'Peter Rabbit' under the low tree branches and as Clay followed, the Sheriff swatted some out of his way, to slap against a sweaty muscular chest. He knew the scriptures, 'There is no greater Love than for a friend to die for a friend," so Nathan was slowing down Clay, on purpose, no way, he was a lawman, a lawman who knew his ex-friend was making HIS GIRL Wendy Lou strawberry ice cream in the kitchen and eating it in the bedroom.

"She will have Clay's babies not yours," a dark opportunist imp.

"Oh gawd help me, I do not want this job as guide as digging a hole in the lower dark energy levels for myself, I just want to go home, boohoo," and did not snort grunt or oink as a sudden calmness became me and an inner strength to rip off my frontage and holler my commitment to save my Sheriff, and did not look at Clay, he was not my responsibility and could be killed and eaten by the dark crazy killer, hey, no one knows he is a crazy killer, oh, I forgot the scalp, yucky, ugly man what are you an ugly man who stuffed himself into 6 sizes to small 'Y' Fronts tiger print, no wonder you *"squeak, titter chuckle and no oink, thank you God."*

And settling down from my name calling found Sheriff Bottom did not look to see if Clay was stopped, as that would **be tempting,** starting to drool over a tanned gymnast, *'grunts'* back.

"Where did the lawmen go?"

"Not telling you," Joseph being a stinker.

"Rattle hiss," sounds vanishing into the bush as dark imps neared and no mouth organ music as the player did not want that strange man to follow his music and whatever to him, scalp, bash him about, pull his knickers off while he was still in them, poke the eyes and pull out the tongue.
Where did I get these wicked thoughts.

"Memories of physical life," and I denied being a pole dancer that mugged her victims, I went to church every Sunday, *"yes after the Saturday night muggings,"* Number Two, got excited as had memories as a physical watching a pole dancer dance, so burst into flames and ran into the Ether, *"I am sorry, forgive me,"* and just like that only a smoldering angel was seen coming back being healed with every step.

CHAPTER 8 THE MELODIOUS SOURCE.

Cindy Lou

Or the Owner of the Melodious repeating tuneful song that all the forest animals knew by heart and sang is met at last, or maybe next year.

Yes, the forest was alive with 'The Sound of Music' so it became an extra sunny day for Alaska, it got a tenth day of sunshine.

"Boys, on a day like this there is nothing to be afraid of, look at the Varied Thrush and the Great Horned Owl watching that thrush, both full of life-giving sunshine," but the lawmen ignored me and did that mean Clay Eagle heard me to, well Rattle Snake Kid I mean Snake Rattle was repeating my words, SO ALL THE RESPONSIBILITY OF FAILURE WOULD BE MINE ALONE, the skunk.

"Sheriff look," Clay being taller and having no low branches in his eyes saw they were at the bottom of a mountain, and there are over a hundred towering mountains, the boys were lost?

"Denali the biggest," Joseph to be smart.

"It is Mount Colville Sheriff," we can climb to the top," Clay.

I looked at Joseph and he shrugged; a mountain was a mountain.

"What do we do when we get to the top Clay," Sheriff Bottom smaller than the small rocks in his way to the top, never mind the Golden Eagle and Bald Eagle savoring his small size seeing him as a tasty bunny.

"Get a birds eye view of Colville City Sheriff and see what has been happening without us, it is the 4th July, gobbler burger time, hope some left at Little Joes," and the Sheriff looked at Clay as if he was an idiot. There better be a good reason to climb to the peak of this mountain.

And Bottom was tired, thirsty hungry and the sun was going down soon so if anything, they needed back to the police patrol vehicle and town.

But Big Foot were pushing them this way, **why, it was a secret.**

And the reasons to climb became obvious, **the stranger appeared** at the other end of the clearing waving an axe, for he figured he could not cut himself up like he had with the cutthroat with an axe.

The strange man had run out of band aid.
The strange man had lost his cutthroat.

The strange man saw himself in an unbroken mirror and thought the axe made up for the lack of ears. An axe he had already used after scalping Bald Pete whose scalp we had met.

The strange man looked like Big Foot and Nathan Bottom was already a hundred yards up before Deputy Clay had gone one foot.

The strange man did soon be joining them for out of the corner of Clay's eye he noticed several larger than life figures, "escaped gorillas," he said hoping, but it was the stink that reached him that alerted him they were not escaped monkeys from a nearby zoo, and Colville did not have a zoo, apart from the local pet shop **so the strange man smelt more** stink behind him, and when the huge human type hand covered in **fur gripped his right shoulder**, "Were-wolf in Fairbanks, Alaska," he had seen the movie also which meant he had been in Colville, who is this man, our murderer of Cindy Lo, definitely Baldy Pete the Gold Panner. "Wait for me," **the strange man** shouted as if the two lawmen or any sane folk would.

"Garble Oink," the sound of a broken heart and HELL KNOWS NO FURY THAN A SCORNED FEMALE, EVEN A SCORNED FEMALE APE.

YES STRANGE MAN RUN.

So never turned and investigated the human faces of two Big Foot whose intentions towards the stranger we will never know now. Who knows maybe they wanted to welcome him to 'BIG FOOT TERRITORY,' or just eat him.

Now to open a secret, one was her and the other her huge monstrous dad.

It was the same Big Feet pushing our lawmen deep into the **dark woods**.

But what did the stranger whose first impression with

myself had caused a flutter do?

Did he scramble up the mountain face with the lawmen?

Did he freeze out of fear and watch himself eaten, alive as Big Foot wants fresh meat?

Did he warn them he was martial arts expert as the law requires?

Did he pull out a hidden Colt and shot them smelly apes who never used loo paper dead?

Did he take from his pockets 'Reese's Peanut Butter Cookies and scatter them as if throwing a grenade as far from himself as possible so them latrine wafting prehistoric big monkeys did follow the crumbs, and he be safe?

Did he use his cutthroat, no he had lost as his bandaged fingers could not open the blade, nor use a mobile keyboard and have Amazon send a drone with a shiny new one, unused.

Did he wield the axe intended to be wielded on our heroes? Obviously not as the flea tick lice infested furry monsters where still ALIVE.

Did he say 'mummy'?

Yes as his knees quaked.

Did he the hardman stranger with the bald hair as all famous hardmen on television are bald, wee his pants?

Yes he did, a long wee that the Big Foot found interesting, why the human pee was yellow like theirs and smelled pee like theirs and formed a splashing puddle for the Big Foot to wiggle their toes in and LAUGH, yes they were laughing as humanoids so must have a language?

"Did he the tough murderer poop himself like a rustler dangling from a 1864 Wyoming gallows,

Yes he did, and the monkey ape men sniffed and "Smells like us, wonderful," in English and how did these prehistoric Giganotosaurus apes speak US English, which did be telling, **it was a secret?**

Did daddy ape throw the strange man over his shoulder and take him back to his abandoned wedding night?

Hope rose in the bosom of the female Big Foot.

And suddenly these two misunderstood apes were staring at empty red trekking boots that had feet in them a moment ago, and how on Earth did this murderous scumbag vacate those red trekking boots. We did have to ask someone who wears red trekking boots **for the secret.** They are laced halfway up the shin bone and **how is a secret**, maybe Johnny Christy wanted him alive to stand trial?

And mouth organ music filled the air.

"Guess maybe so, so not a secret titter."

*

"I am really p**sed off under these leaves and want up, something edible as starving and a pint of white coffee with sugar as I am not a 'Die Hard Hardman' who can drink scalding coffee without being rushed to emergency, I am a weak female melodious energy level drawing in my lawmen who at least better have a can of 'ice cream soda' on one, and diet caramel fizz drink on the other.

As a pretty melody tune I must watch my figure or will not be 'The Fairest in the Land,' that other melodious pitch 'Sleeping Beauty' will out sing, shine, and romance me.

Hello, who are you, are you Cinderella as you do not have black hair so can not be Sleeping Beauty? Is your hair red, are you from 'Enchanted' and really Cinderella as in that movie you have red hair, if you are any of these two competitors, WHAT DO YOU WANT?

"That is nice, I am Sheriff Nathan Bottom's female beautiful, magnificent, wonderful superwoman witty smart tall BLOND translucent pin up guide if you do not mind, sent here to solve the murders and disappearances as The Alaskan Triangle is giving Alaska the name of 'Monster State.'"

"Well then ghost am I dead or alive as I am not even sure where I am?"

This melody singer **I forgave**, almost as did not want to snort grunt again, she must be fed up lying in that grave covered in leaves, I did be too so would you.

"Well done my dear, grunt snort, you understood her anxieties," Boss Angel needing to understand why he was still 'grunting, snorting, oinking' with an excited wiggly pink tail.

Excited yes, the spirit of the woman in the grave was still attached to her physical body, she was not completely dead.

"Or ever the silver cord be loosed, then shall the dust return to the Earth as it was and the spirit shall return unto God who gave it, Ecclesiastes," Joseph stunning me, he was more than a stupid male guide, he was educated, a plus for interested girl-guides, and I felt a 'grunt' rising in my throat and praised Joseph **for humbling me** and the 'grunt' subsided.

Encouraged, Joseph turned turncoat, for instead of making a snidey remark puffed his chest and threw back his head so the kiss curls I never noticed before wafted gently turning into inviting fingers for me to fall and worship him as a MALE, *'grunt snort grunt oink'* and not from admiration of a male codpiece but female devilish frenzy to rip Joseph into tiny orbs, so anyone seeing them did have to guess which was he, *'titter grunt titter oink, I worship no man.'*

"Are you idiots finished, I mean I am lying in a trench hovering near the ceiling of this darkly lit cave watching them, those big feet covered in fur and what they had been standing in that smells so bad.
Am I dead or living for I see my silver cord is not broken so I must not be dead, oh Gawd one of them critters with those big feet is squatting and, I am not mentioning it, where am buried, in a primitive outhouse, oh no, the fiend is peeing over me, I will pull the 'bl**dy' thingmabob off, if I had hands," the source of the melody and since she was lecturing us guides, had stopped singing, but

not the six hundred song birds, hundred beavers, twenty cougars and a representative of every Alaskan forest animals, she taught them well.

"*Rattle hiss,*" and Snake Rattle managed to do his serpentine ventriloquist act for the animals with BIG FEET who heard and mayhem happened, for snakes is feared, especially them that 'rattle.'

And forty-four male and twenty-four female and ten babies and children all with large feet ran out the cave into Alaskan cloud.

We were in a cave, and those thingamabobs with large feet where what those thingamabobs humans call "BIG FOOT," outside and because they was in a panic over a translucent rattlesnake, and you did think these gorillas did just pick up big stones and squash the rattler, then eat it and there was a small pit glowing red embers, so prehistory must be rewritten whom started using fire.

Anyway.

"Nathan let me help you up over this last ridge, then we are up and I smell smoke, strange?" Clay Eagle afraid of a forest fire behind them but he smelt gobbler burger, "How is that possible?"

"*Oh, Clay whatever you do, do not bend down as the answer is coming?*" I warned him but because I was not his official spirit guide he did not listen, and I was a female, so Clay's Tarzan shape lost some appeal.

"*V' fingered him,*" I easily remembered the fingers from our side of life.
So deserved what came.

"*Oh, Sheriff Bottom, whatever you do, do not take Clay's*

outstretched hand of offered help to pull you up and over the last edge, please."

"Gants even way up here," was his reply as figured without ghosts chattering in his head, he did have no psychiatric problems, so did not listen, the burke so, "F***k' him."

"Grunt snort oink," and was Joseph as a lesson to be a neutral guide, not a male pink wiggly thingamabob that he and Boss Angel grew just like that in a POOF, there it was, a piggy tail.

"I never suffer headaches for I am who I am and regret guides, do animals have guides, I am not telling as is funny listening to humans debate that, but you lot have given me a thunderstorm, see the clouds darkening." Which guide thought this?

"Hey, Sheriff, is that your hairy furry hands on my bum Sheriff Bottom," Clay Eagle thinking you could work with someone and call your Boss friend, and twenty years later find he was a gay person, then remembered his friend did not have hairy furry hands as he was holding his hands, so whose hairy furry hands were on his bottom.

So, Clay Eagle worried now.

Did the strange man have big furry hairy hands?

If so, then Clay Eagle should be more than worried.

Was there band aid and stitches on those more than big hairy furry hands?

If so, Clay Eagle was about to go to his Happy Hunting ground in the sunset coming, then Clay did not need to worry who owned those hairy fury palms as he did be amongst the bison and not a single European seen.

Was there an almighty stink left on his bottom as those hairy furry fingers needed a wash as has been used with leaves as toilet paper, thus explaining the stench of these legendary mythical creatures.

If so, Clay better change places with Nathan Bottom as it says, 'There is no Greater love than to lay down your life for a friend,' and the question was?

Did Nathan regard Clay highly enough to change places.

If so, then why was the sheriff peeling off Clay's hands to be free of his friends grasp.

Friends for over twenty years, must get boring and need a face change?

If so, that explains why Sheriff Nathan fell backwards with a yelp and "What have I done, that was my best friend I left with them monkeys, correction, Big Footers," as Nathan was looking at them, whereas Clay was showing them his bottom, with dirty finger stains on his moons smelling of pooh.

If so, Medium Wendy Lou who did his washing did use those deputy expensive trousers as barbecue fuel, expensive as bought in a Montana Gift Shop.

"Sheriff, it is me, your guide Betty Lou come to save you," and the poor falling man, as you pick up speed as you fall you know, looked at me as if he was speaking to an idiot, well I never.

"And as the owner of the melody I can see all as am floating outside my body and am not dead as still am attached to my body by my silver cord and should never have built hopes of rescue when seeing who was doing the rescuing, boohoo."

"Sheriff catch me," as Clay sped past his friend Nathan who obviously did not believe in, "There is no greater love than to lay down your life for a friend."

"What is holding your bum?" Our Sheriff Nathan curiously asks as there are two gigantic gorilla type monkeys holding Clay's fake alligator P.V.C. belt, as Clay did not like trophy hunting, and it was the belt the fury hairy fingers had been checking out, and Clay slipped out and mumbled, "EEK," as he fell into clean fresh Alaskan air leaving stinks behind.

Rattle, yes if it had been real alligator skin, these ferocious almost extinct animals did have ripped Clay up and shared him with their friends as they believed still in the virtues of friendship, unlike Sheriff Bottom who had not changed place topside.

"Rattle."

"Yes?"

"Shut up," I told him and put the fingers in his empty sockets as he was a spirit guide made of Mind and Light and whatever?

That also explains why Clay went fast in descent because of the greater weight mass of him, whereas Nathan being a small squirt floated down like a feather, taking time to somersault and do back flips and wave at the Big Foot above on the ledge watching the exciting action below.

And they threw the fake P.V.C. belt after them.

*

And below **a strange man** panting up the mountain side as was exhausted running for his life going up that steep mountain side, sometimes slipping on stuff thrown out topside, so his band aid covered fingers soon became covered in rotten food remains, and some Big Foot above, smarter than its kin, and fed up of the phew pongs above, having watched Johnny Christie sneaking about the woods, and drunk Friday night visitors to Little Joes after closing time, full of gobbler burgers relief themselves in the **dark woods**.

To a watching unseen Big Foot this was marvelous, so copied and squatted over the edge high above watched by curious hairy friends, who joyed as their stink was somewhere else.

On band aid hands, which rubbed the sweat and grim from a strangers eyes and mouth.

"What the hell is this stuff, 'Christ' it is not, is it, 'Christ it is,'" and this fink should not be uttering such a name, but notice did not add 'Son of God' so could be any 'Christ,' perhaps short for Johnny Christie?

What gives with Johnny Christie and this strange murderer? It is a secret.

Then "rattle" and was not Snake rattle who was busy saying Native American Last Rites for Clay Eagle speeding down towards the fink below.

"Get lost," the fink and grabbed the rattle and threw the venomous snake away, except it had its fangs sunk in his leather belt pumping lethal yellow venom out, that seeped towards import jewels.

So preoccupied were these two, human and reptile, human to pull his underwear off while he wore trousers, as they was seeped in venom that would ruin his TOTAL WELLBEING, understand? And the venomous serpent wanted him dead, so either did not hear "WOSH" and Clay Eagle landed on both, flattening, well, squashing the bad snake that slithered away, happy to disappear from this awful tale.

But not so the fink, knocked and winded cold.

"I must give the kiss of life as think I killed this mountaineer?" Clay Eagle remembering his mail order first aid course, a pity the course did not provide actual hands-on bodies, or Clay would have asked.

Is the body breathing.
Is there blue about the lips mistaking the deep purple lipstick as deep vein blood, Clay's fault, he had landed on this half naked stranger in the woods, and did he ask why this man was almost

naked?

Is that tattoos with 'I love Bald Pete' on his left chest and 'I scalped you cheater,' on his right chest, and 'Johnny Christie is the best' across the tummy and never mind, all censored and did IT CLICK IN CLAY EAGLE'S HEAD this man was the murderer as they had stupidly thrown away a scalp further down the mountain as being 'YUCKY' and 'GERM RIDDEN,' but to give the deputy leeway, his head was full of Snake Rattle's confusing *'rattle.'*

"My friend Sheriff Nathan Bottom whom I have served over twenty years is right, he and I are schizophrenics needing put away in an asylum for mentally disturbed lawmen, with television, scrumptious food, nurses in Halloween Nurse outfits as society knows how to repay lawmen who SERVED and PROTECTED society.

"Away in your dreams Clay," I shouted at the dreamer.

Is there broken bones sticking out from limbs?

And wondered not why there were so many band aids and bandages on this almost naked stranger? Maybe the stranger had an argument with a motorcycle lawless gang, maybe 'Demon Angels' who scowl the Alaska Motorways hoping to catch a Big Foot and claim rewards such as advertising 'Wonder Knickers For Girl Motorcyclists' and 'Harley Morrisons sun powered razor to shave while driving,' and not get killed as the razor levitates itself with A1 intelligence.

Is that a silver dog tag about his neck, no, it is a rainbow condom full of Viagra blue tablets.

And the watching silent guides were beginning to wonder about Clay?

"Rattle," went Clay's guide Snake Rattle, which was helpful.

"Hey, Clay is that you?" Clay heard a shout and thought the 'Thunderbird' of legend had come to eat him for who else would know his name up here on this cold mountain face? The forgetful idiot was so preoccupied in resuscitating the mysterious stranger he had landed on to provide him a soft landing, he had forgotten his friend falling to meet him at 70 mph they say you fall, then it doubles so 'wow,' Sheriff Bottom was to hit Clay at 140 m.p.h. good grief, actually something stronger is needed, Good Gawd save the idiot as there is no one else to save the melodious song and allow all the forest animals trapped in that tune to escape, back to their daily lives, of hunting and eating each other, just like we guides did once to each other in THE HUMAN SUBWAY JUNGLE, before the crowd shoved us onto oncoming trains, or was stalked and mugged violently that we woke up here with Number Two Angel rifling our pockets for identification.

Or in confusion that our bed partner was in bed not with me, but them noisy neighbors, you walked across the road when the GREEN MAN was a RED MAN, and woke up here with Boss Angel asking why you are up here and not down there where it is flaming hot?

No wonder we never guided Nathan to glide 20 degrees south and miss Clay and not cause bodily grievous harm to Clay.

But the stranger awoke, saw Clay, and CENSORED but Clay rolled away spitting and brushing his teeth with fallen acorns and big grubs by mistake that looked like leafy twigs, and was violently ill with these words of wisdom, "That definitely was not Madam Wendy Lou," and was smelly and looked green and was on his fours retching.

"*Rattle,*" Snake rattle telling Clay to get up and run as that was a silly position while a strange, excited man with naughty criminal intent was tugging at his belt.

"Rattle," Snake rattle.

Speak Americano and this modern Native American will understand, oh I could waste time as had no ideas myself but was obvious Snake rattle could not speak American.

"Yah, yes, no, maybe," Snake rattle understanding and indicated these were his modern American words he understood as taught them two hundred years ago, and he is a guide?

"What about you dear?" And was Number Two lifting up my translucent smock to show ankles with bangles and a hippy flute tucked in them, and was that weed?

Point made.

And what saved Clay Eagle, not guides sent by heaven that was for sure, but the VENOM on the belt made the stranger's band aid fingers numb and Sheriff Bottom landed on him.
AMEN.

And missing mouth organ music filled the air.

*

Knocked the strange, man unconscious so unknown to the lawmen, the stranger visited Minus Level Three Heaven where Stain Paul did not visit, as Saint Paul went upstairs to Level Three, (can be verified St. James bible and other versions.) this man went down three levels and conversed not with angels but the opposite, and learned nasty things to do to our lawmen when he awoke, and he awoke with a big grin, that sparkled gold fillings, gold stolen from Baldy Pete the Gold Panner who met an unfortunate end, he was scalped.

"He is alive, Yippy Yahoo Ride Them Hug Them Brand

Them," one of our idiots, can you guess which one.

"Clay, shut up and let us question this lost tourist as to how he got lost?" Sheriff Bottom.

"How did you get lost up here almost naked, I heard some mountains do that to you, has the spirit of the mountain affected you?" Clay and Nathan did not look at him as if he were affected mentally with stress, as he knew all about voices in the head, and besides, this was ALASKA.

Now the **strange man**, since I am a ghostly guide read his mind so, *"Joseph, this man plans to kill our lawmen, well especially the small ugly one and keep the beautiful, snort grunt, one captive, warn them Joseph, grunt and had to retreat to clear my mind of snorts and grunts and too many male chests about, with nothing on, titter, oink, of Gawd I am sorry I was born a woman."*
And my mind cleared but in those few seconds what we call time had moved on.
Joseph if that was him, the strange man who had sprung up like a mountain lion with Big Foot blood and were-wolf shape changer genes in him, to thump Sheriff Bottom on the head with a clenched fist, then pull his lugs wide, poke his eyes with band aid fingers, pull the sheriff's tongue out with those filthy fingers, and twist that tongue here and there, then knee the poor sheriff in the mouth but thankfully our Sheriff is so small was kneed in the forehead and saved an expensive dental bill.

"Hi Yaa Watha," Clay Eagle said coming out of his shock that had demobilized him of action man activity.

"Hi Yaa Watha," the strange man imitating Clay then beat the monkey sh*t out of Clay.

"*Rattle*," Snake Rattle trying to frighten the attacker away.

"*What is wrong with Clay?*" I was amazed my muscular Tarzan shaped Native American was not losing his temper, any sane person would have picked up the rattle and thrown it on the attacker.

"Rattle?" Yes there was one between the two men.

"*Clay is a pacifist Betty Lou,*" Snake Rattle between the rattles.

"*A F****ing what?*" I asked dumfounded, well you learn new things every day, but "*Clay Dear, clench your fists and stick out your arms so you hit the fink in the eyes, blinding him, so you can high kick him next, then blow in his face so he falls flat.*" That is what I call advice.

"Rattle."

I looked and was not sure if that snake between the two men was a spirit guide or a venomous serpent.
And it bit the big stranger in the place he needs for making babies, so was a real snake.

And Clay picked up his fallen friend, and how these two could still be friends is anyone's guess and climbed the mountain.

Back to the source of song where animals waited on cracks and crannies, tree branches and treetops for the melody to start again.

And at the source big furry creatures waited for Clay too.

If he had only listened he did have heard the bugle of scouts, firemen bagpipes, and floats below coming his way and gone towards them.

Folk unable to watch our lawmen been thrown off a mountain edge, attacked by a strange man, well that was their version as was below and needed binoculars to see the truth, but did not have any, just as well, as had changed their opinion of our boys, **they were heroes.**

Those were Big Foot murderers up there and that strange man must be an accomplice to the murderers, yes, all idiots.

"Rattle."
Real or that guide?

CHAPTER 1 BOOK 2

Betty Lou the spirit guide, cur blimey I
thought they looked like nuns,
but she was a cowgirl, 'rope them, ride them, brand them.'

And the fire chief saw a clearing, a mountain meadow full of flowers and small animals playing, and fallen tree trunks from vicious winter snowstorms, lucky it was summer then?

A mountain stream gurgled invitingly for clear drinking water, as this high up should be no polluted latrine waste from luggers, gold panners, tourists, Big Foot hunters and paranormal experts and television crews and the cooking cruiser and sleeper and fly tippers, but they were wrong, Big Foot had copied HER/HIS human elders and saw the stream higher up as a toilet flush, but not a bottom wash so explains why Big Foot still stank, and also, if they learned from humans, folk they saw were unhygienic as not cleaning the hands and that place that stinks Big Foot passed all the intestinal colic, worms, diphtheria, dysentery and cholera germs into that crystal clear stream that became a river below full of salmon, grizzly bears fishing, and tourists sneaking up behind the grizzly bears to make trophies of them bears and salmon.

Do not fret, the trophy hunters vanished as this was the Alaskan Triangle and full of red baboons and creatures with big beaks and vanishing tourists so the bears were safe.

"Let us resume?" The Fire Chief meaning?

"Yes, it is still 4th and gobbler burger day," takes another.

"Hey Farmer Sam, did you and your boys carry up the barbecue grills?" Number three.

"Hey Little Joe, did you bring up the girls" another.

"The alcohol fool," another.

"Did the lawyer come?" A wife representing wives and girlfriends for greedy divorce settlements.

"The town militia got the self-assembly log cabins?" Another.

"I brought a movie projector," another.

"I got guns in case of monsters," another and was crowded out with folk wanting GUNS.

"Puff pant here we sanitation boys and girls carried up a solar panel generator, wheeze," tired sanitation workers.

"I got a marque selling emporium wonder goods at discount," a cousin of little Joe.

And I looked for their guides to encourage these town people to come higher and recue the lawmen.

"Are you kidding, Big Foot lives up there, as guides and article

17 it is our job to guide them to safety, so staying put, besides, "Big Foot Meets the Alaskan Pony Express," *is showing and hear a generator thumping away, good night Madam,"* a guide looking like a guardian angel, or thought he/she was, and I could have materialized strangling hands but heard, *"They have a job to do snort,"* and was Boss Angel reminding me of my job and noticed he was covering his mouth, I wonder what he was holding in, so moved to find my boys and heard faintly, "SNORT GRUNT OINK."

And as I drifted up with an up going warm breeze I saw heaven opened and Saint Paul's Level Three Light Zone, and understood a secret of heaven, **'say you are sorry,'** and realized why when I asked for forgiveness with an apology my 'grunts, snorts and oinks' went.

So shouted that back to Boss Angel who was snorting amongst fallen acorns.

I called again, maybe he heard, but know Number Two did for he stood in the path of my thought projection and smiled nodding his head and felt his satisfaction that he was going to try it out and be the NEW BOSS angel, oh heaven help us.

Then darkness mingled with me as dark imps chattering like monkeys with wings, passed me, seeing me threw fruit skins and rolled up 'Boys Magazines' at me and horrified saw me in a thermal swimsuit as a pin up, the dirty naughty advisors to bad humans.

Mind you, I looked stunning, and they had blown up my melons a bit and overdone the red lipstick, and 'grunt.'

So, mellowing out rested.

So, did not see **the stranger reach our lawmen** with a weapon, **a chainsaw.**

So, did not recognize the weapons as a discarded lumber jack tool, **a chainsaw.**

So, was it an electric or petrol stinky two stroke motor type and working or just for show to terrify the lawmen the **chainsaw.**

So, our lawmen went bogle eyed and filled with "I do not want to die," "I am too young to die," "I want my Wendy Lou," "Wendy Lou, you know her to well?" "You been watching drive in movies with her too?" "We are no ,longer friends." "I am going my way; you go that way." "Fine by me man who is no longer my friend." "I will get a new Native American Deputy." "I can be any American Sheriff's Deputy as have twenty years' experience with a nut case who left his Santa red and white socks in her bed, and was you, friend," "I know she preferred me than you, eating dry crackers in bed leaves itchy crumbs," "makes the mare jump about, try it some time," "Mm, I ate a garlic gob sucker before WE READ 'The Adventures of Puss and Boots in Alaska' as the garlic stench makes Wendy Lou jump here and there like an Olympic athlete."

And Joseph listened and learned, and next reincarnation would apply this rotten trick in bed with Whoever Lou reading the Sunday Comic Strips.

So, was no wonder they ran into furry hands that held them out over a mountain ledge, so were now captives and looked down, and were ill, as everything below was small moving specks in a mountain meadow, and the sounds of a were-wolf howling in the flicks was heard, an extra in the movie, 'Big Foot Meets The Pony Express in Alaska.'

Mathematically it took forty-six seconds for the illness from two grown men to reach the happy movie watchers below, who demanded who had been sick on them, and never looked above so bruised themselves with fold down chairs, soft burger buns, plastic fizzy drink bottles and filled diapers, and needed an angel to visit them and encourage forgiveness.

"Oh, Boss Angel where art thou?"
"Grunt snort."

"I will go as know all about praying for forgiveness so can teach these angry people and point their anger towards two lawmen," Number Two, and was he being a Number Two, and he went while superior watching angels watched.

And not all the smelly illness wafted all the way to the joyful picnickers but splattered across **a strange man's face.**

"I am blinded," he said unafraid of The Big Foot **and why was he not afraid?**

"Hello Mr. Henderson," a Big Foot called in, in English, how, **was it a secret**, yes?

"Bye Mr. Henderson," another peeved not getting free frozen chops.

"I could have grabbed his hands but he jilted me, buy lover," yes it was her, Miss Gilgamesh Big Foot and true to his words, "I am blinded," missed his stepping and with a horrible screech fell away, the warmup lifting breeze not being a winter gale was unable to blow him upright.

"Bye fink," I shouted after him and his departing dark imps.

And as the two lawmen were carried away to the pot:

"I am sorry I ate brownie fudge cherry pie with Wendy Lou Clay, hope we are friends again?"
"I am sorry Nathan I ate vindaloo vegan beaver curry with Wendy Lou, hope we are friends again?

"I am sorry I ate roast duck with Cindy Lou from Little Joes as I know you fancied her," Sheriff Bottom not happy Clay his good friend ate a hot vindaloo beaver curry with Wendy Lou.

"Roast duck with Cindy Lou?" Clay aghast, he was wanting that duck with Wendy Lou, and wondered if they were friends.

"And took her on vacation when I won a free holiday to New York Zoo last summer, and you were promoted to Temporary Sheriff so could not come along as extra travel bags," Nathan hoping the temporary promotion did pacify his new enemy.

"Well, I took Wendy Lou to Disney World Paris with my reward money from catching the illegal Fairbanks Moonshine Girls Brigade," Clay retaliating.

"Is that your child Wendy Lou sent to live with her parents?" Nathan and felt bad?

"I am a dad, she never told me, I thought she was eating too much ROAST DUCK," a war was looming, where were the guides?

Well, there was me listening to mouth organ music and Joseph was studying the Big Foot as his old country Poland had only were-wolf legends, so was amazed these monkeys were not in a pet shop.

"*Rattle,*" and explains a lot about Snake rattle.

And without warning Clay exploded with wrath and jumped Nathan who likewise was a tempest of betrayal, and missed each other, as the small one went through Clay's legs to hit upon the hairy legs of a Big Foot, a female big Foot that picked up Nathan Bottom, made baby sounds, and stuck her greasy thumb into his mouth to suck.

And Clay came to a stop against the hanging parts of a big male Big Foot.

"Slave are we?" The ape in good American.

Clay pointed at Nathan his best friend and nodded.

A reply was a grunt and huge hands picked him up and threw him into a hole filled with leaves, and as he flew into the vegetation he noticed, **"They do have big feet."**

Then he landed and sank and disappeared and still managed to breath as the leaves were lose, then stopped sinking, he had come to rest on something cold.

"A sleeping rattler," his first thoughts until calming he groped with huis hands and felt, "Melons," he shouted and immediately stopped groping as he was a decent man.

And the melodious singing started again, under Clay so he was naturally petrified.

"Where art thou friend Nathan," Clay trying to rise but that meant using his experienced hands to push himself up, and yes experienced hands as had read 'Moby Whale,' with Wendy Lou and one hundred 'Bugs Bunny Rabbit' comics with Cindy Lou, and never attended any anatomy university classes.

"He was a pervert, a fink," I shouted then stopped, I had never attended any medical courses and knew what a weenie was titter and did not grunt as humor exists my side.

And the mouth organ music got louder so all the Big Foot hairy people gathered near the edge to listen, as was spell bound.

The noise of a chain saw heard as it was wrapped about

an Alaskan Cedar a thousand feet below and from it a stranger somersaulted, danced over the chain saw, dived under it, kicked it, and cursed the idiot for filling the Two Struck Tank for the chainsaw could Samba for the next six hours.

Maybe **the snake bites did finish the stranger first?**

Or the chain saw wrapped itself about him and dice him up into bite sized red baboon eatables?

Or it might start raining and water and electricity do not mix, electrocuting the stranger thus saving American citizens the expense of locking him away fed on Corn Flakes and porridge for sixty years.

Or the Big Foot did rescue their Mr. Henderson, **their?**
Or the picnickers did hear the nosy chain saw that was spoiling the rest of the movie 'Big Foot Meets the Alaskan Pony Express,' as their heated vicious frontier brawl had passed off as an ICE CREAM break.

Were friends became friends again and drank bottled alcohol and eyed the women towns folk, married, divorced, single, elderly who threw away their empty alcohol bottles and line danced while mouth organ music drifted down to them, giving them beat.

Tonight, there might be murder here, lawmen were needed, and where were ours?

*

"Things is not all that bad, look I get to look after the baby and get fed when baby gets fed, the only drawback is I am the babies toy," Sheriff bottom and with that became a stress doll as baby Big Foot pulled, poked, tore and threw and when Bottom bounced back jumped gleefully.

And when Bottom did not bounce back, well to stop baby Big Foot screaming mamma would kick Bottom back.

Then baby had teething problems and Bottom decided he was wrong, "See we can admit such a crucial decision, in this case, things were bad, he needed to escape before that dummy of a baby bit something Wendy Lou liked as a nighttime surprise.

The problem was how to escape.

There were many Big Foot about and knew what to do with an escapee, give him back to baby.

And help was coming, a barbarian horde of towns folk were ascending the mountain to help their lawmen.

"To lynch them," Mother Cindy Lou still hoping for a necktie party when moonshine flowed and men saw her as an attractive beauty.

"Why some men carried barrels full of XXX.
Why some men carried a movie projector.
Why some men carried films tins.
Big Foot married my cousin Sarah Lou,
Big Foot was just a few hundred meters more
Climbing.
Big Foot did not welcome uninvited folks.
Big Foot threw rocks and tree trunks to soften you
up,
As eating you raw was tough going.
But help was on the way,
In more ways than one," Mountain Goats illuminating you of proceedings 'bray, bray.'

In more ways than one was the stranger, him, the dark man having heard a melody feared his game was up and he did be lynched by them lot scrambling up the rocks below.

"You have found me,
   My charming prince,
      Kiss me quick." The melody went and meant one of them law boys had found the source of that irritating Disney flop song.

And the thousand songbirds, squirrels, racoons, bears, elks, moose, monsters not mentioned here, all sang,

"Clay is his name Cindy Lou,
   Muscular and handsome.
      He will not save you as is
         Pacifist,
            Get the shrimp instead," yes the animals of Alaska had been following this ridiculous tale so gave Cindy Lou good advice.

So, an incensed broken hearted strange man jumped from rock top to rock top, from cedar top to swing to the next treetop, and he hollered, "Arrrrrrrrrgh," in imitation of hardmen who do such things such as Tarzan.

But he was no 'Die Hard or Ape humanoid,' he was a fink instead and proved it as a treetop swung back between his legs so the tough bald strange made funny faces, then allowed the treetop to catapult him high in the sky, where a passing Bald Eagle pecked a few toes off as was hungry, pitiful thing.

And falling back to earth fast as he was a heavy sod, a lost Andean Condor ate the remaining toes.

Where were his red trekking boots to stop this bird feeding, well he vacated them earlier which means he has been walking about bare footed.

Just wait **till he ever** sneaks into Medium Wendy Lou's

antiseptic cleaned sparkling floor as she used, 'Mr. Sparkle' multi wash, for floors and toilet stains.

Maybe he was sneaking in as seems he knew Colville well.

How well did Granny Cindy Lou know him?

Did he guzzle moonshine and see her and Mother Cindy Lou as beautiful girls, remember beauty is skin deep.

We will never know as girls never reveal that type of **secret**.

*

"Friend Nathan come save me a zombie has me, a Walking dead, oh Tonka I convert," but he was already a new Age Red Man so that did not work.

A woman was standing next to him with leaves, rubbish and Big Foot stink stuck to her, so Clay looked her over before checking himself for stuff sticking to him.

"That is some woman in front of me and I recognize her as not only ate vindaloo beaver with Wendy Lou, but Skunk Chow Mein with Cindy here, and my exploring hands told me, yes she is Cindy Lou, and why has she just knocked a tooth out of me.

"Never paw a woman uninvited sonny, giggle."

And it had taken Clay's arrival, his warmth, his energy, his human contact to vitalize Cindy Lou who had imagined she was trapped under all that well, household waste.

"You are alive," Clay finding it hard to pronounce words with a new gap in his front teeth.

Cindy Lou peeled a skinny rodent tail from her teeth.

Clay looked at his feet, cute rodents were every where wanting him to take them home as pets.

Then Cindy Lou bent down and retrieved a fizzy drink can and drank and offered Clay, "Drink," it was a command, do as we do, 'When in Rome behave as a Roman,' as not to offend and Clay did not want to offend Cindy Lou whom he hoped to have more Elk Brazilian barbecued ribs with, so drank.

He spat most of it out.

"Big Foot pee, kept me hydrated."
Clay retched over Cindy Lou and a tooth.
"This was some brutal woman, what did Clay see in her?"

"Well, she is the town dentist and I know what Clay sees in her," Joseph smirking.
"The pervert, the son of Fili Pek."

And was Cindy Lou taking Clay by a hand took him to the cave mouth and seeing Bottom entertaining the Big Foot by being kicked to the baby back and forth, decided to run for it.

"What about my friend?" Clay asked.
"Remember Wendy, rattle."

That was his excuse for deserting Sheriff Nathan Bottom who believed *'there is no greater love than to give your life for a friend,'* so the friends can have Wendy Lou, Cindy Lou and all the other girls not mentioned here or it did take up thirty volumes of books.

*

Now some say Big Foot and critters walk through a portal allowing prehistoric animals into our world.

Others that they are aliens.
Others paranormal finks.

Whatever it is advised not to feed them, but he did, **the stranger.**

And Sheriff Bottom seeing Clay and 'a woman' sneaking into

the **dark woods** went crazy, and what saved him from being eating because the baby Big Foot started crying was a vial of pheromones that used to belong to a strange man dropped out of his back pocket and bust open.

Sheriff Bottom smelled rotten dried fish.
The Big Foot smelled LOVE.

A jilted member of the ape tribe snatched Sheriff Bottom and ran into the **dark woods** with him heading towards the summit.

The female Big Foot looked familiar, obviously had not learned a lesson about dating humans.

The same direction as Clay and Cindy Lou.

"Does no one in this rotten tale head down, help is down, Colville is down, Mother Cindy Lou with a necktie is down, so head up boys, giggle."

"And you are going with them both," was Boss Angel and gulping I went as noticed he might have not snorted but there was a pink wiggly thingy poking places at the back, I was being a good girl guide.

Then the strange man fell upon the gathering, yes fell as he had come up higher. This is what happened: *"Rattle,"* they get everywhere so losing his balance he fell down and was caught by a father of a jilted Big Foot, a father who was glad to see him, son-in-law, grunt.

"Tee he," the idiot said to the ape, then as quick as his too tight 'Y' fronts allowed him he was gone, how did he do that.

I mean there was disease spreading ape saliva drooling over his face.

An ape was digging dirty oak hardened fingernails into his bum.

"Where is the chops faggot?" His ex-daddy-in-law asked.

A jilted Big Foot girl was thinking of ditching Bottom and rekindling a romance with the strange man.
Whom would she chose?

She dropped Bottom, well tossed him aside and went after the strange man.

But the strange man was gone going the same way as the Clay and one girl.

"ROAR," and a roar from the assembled Big Foot.

"I heard nothing," Mother Cindy Lou lying as she wanted a lynching at the top.
Guzzling of moonshine and gnashing of cold stale gobbler burgers heard covered in mayo that made the burger eatable.

They were going up.

Anyway, "Sheriff I was coming to look for you," Clay lying finding his ex-friend ahead where he had landed.

"And Sheriff Bottom recognized Cindy Lou and gave her his clothes to wear except his pants.
"What a gentleman."

And as she dressed into tiny trousers she managed to stand on Clay's toes many times, wiggle a bum into him so he fell over onto poisonous toadstools and soon would be warty, in all places and need the cottage hospital, and be mended so do not worry female followers, your Clay will be bright as new.

And managed while he wore them took his 'Y' spotless white fronts from him and dangled his extra-large cod piece.
"You fraud," Sheriff Bottom and she tossed it away.

A faint giggle escaped Clay.

Then the escaped strange man arrived.

"Who hit me with this," he said holding up the cod piece. Full of confidence as knew Clay was a pacifist and the other a shrimp, and Cindy again his prisoner.
Then the aliens arrived, yes, it was strange lights in the sky.
Then the Big Feet arrived smelling the place up.
Then the Colville Mob arrived drunk as usual.
Then the avalanche happened.

None were transported to safety aboard the alien ship.
All were washed away gaining speed as they went.

"Wee," Granny Cindy Lou showing thigh and the drunks thought she was beautiful.

"Daughter?" Mother Cindy Lou hiding the necktie behind her as how could she hang these lawmen now; they had rescued her daughter.

"Mine," the strange man and grabbed Cindy Lou but that necktie was loose and went about his neck, and they were rushing by Cedar trees at 10 m.p.h. as an avalanche takes time to get speedy.

"Lover," and it was his ex-Big Foot fiancé holding the other end of the necktie.

"Giggle, honey I can explain," but she was a jilted ape.

And the avalanche went silent as the **dark woods** wanted to know what the ape would do.

"She speaks English?" Mother Cindy Lou amazed and **was a secret** so was not answered.

And the jilted broken-hearted ape held the end of the necktie tightly as their speed had increased to 12 m.p.h.

"Gulp," **the strange man** seeing his fate if he did not do some quick thinking, but thinks quick in a situation like this, I know graduates from West Point and Sandhurst Military Academies, but the strange man was not one of their graduates so his brain fizzled for answers.

"Marry her sonny," Granny Cindy Lou loving weddings as men at parties drank more moonshine and married her.

"How many times are you married Granny?" I asked not expecting an answer.

"She has twenty husbands," Boss Angel and not divorced once.
"You mean she is a giggle?"
"Yes, bigamist snort."

Then the avalanche fed up with the lot of them took a detour and avoided the treetops as there were nesting woodpeckers there, and all found themselves sailing in the Alaskan fresh air.

Without a patrol car to land in.

"Oh, Sweet Jesus I am dead," was Father Cindy Lou in a wheelchair and guzzled a whole bottle of moonshine so passed out.

Oblivious to his fate.

"Question is, would Sweet Jesus save him, he was living in Little Joes while his wife lived across the backyards? Titter."

"Oh, great Tonka show yourself and carry me to the ground," Clay and would Tonka save him, did he dance in the reservations to Tonka, nope, he watched drive in movies with girls.

"Oh, Great Sheriff in The Sky, save your servant Nathan Bottom," and *"giggle there is no Great Sheriff in the Sky idiot, so he was a dead man, giggle."*

"Oh, save me," *"the strange man never been in a religious house since a baby, so had no one to ask to save him, but he had forgotten he followed one, was he afraid now that he was about DIE? Nope, he was so arrogant."*

"Oh Lord it is me, Mother Cindy Lou, save me from being swashed," *"and did not say please as was assured Sundays by the pastor she was saved."*

"I do not need saving with all these drunk men, what a way to go out," Granny Cindy Lou guzzling moonshine as an anesthetic.
"I was saved for this, surely I am deemed for better things?" And Cindy Lou was heard and an upward gust slowed all of their decent down to 5 m.p.h.

She had suffered enough pain to gain salvation.

True, a storyteller never tells porkers, fibs, lies, always what a storyteller see, hears, and feels, when sober of course.

"It had to be Boss Angel snort who liked a pretty ankle and Cindy

Lou had them even in Sheriff Bottoms small clothes fit for a garden gnome," and I got 'snort' back for cheek, heaven was getting strict with me, would I ever learn, *"Lord take me as I am, there are many colors of bugs, fish, and humans, so I am what I am, a cheek artist, sorry, and the snort went."*

"I am saved, *thank you lord, I have so much faith I do not need this,"* the pastor and lucky those stitches he could not rip out under sticky bandages for his stomach bullet wound, but did kick his heels and jump high in happiness as he had firm ground under him, "Bl***Y Cat what you drop here?" As what he stood in was soft and squelchy but then, clutched his stomach and collapsed in pain, and was ignored, and that is what he got for bigotry as was not that mangy cat but stuff raining down from some of the fallers, Big Foot folks that did not exist.

Them that landed on him squelching him further into the squelch.

Big Foot each weighing 600 lbs. and there were many, including the broken-hearted female who took an interest in the pastor, peeling him up so she could have a good sniff, and decided he she did not like his after shave so gently let him down, patted him and went after her tribe grunting, heading for trash cans and moldy gobbler burgers, garlic doughballs, vindaloo wraps and spaghetti as they liked the stringy ringed tails Chef used to put meat in his dishes.
"Chef?

Hell Fire, with all the moonshine and frolicking no one wanted a pastor about so left him, so where did the rescued go, **a secret***, no not all as look there they go, some punching their neighbors, some converting their neighbors wallets,*
Some coveting the neighbors wife,
Others coveting the grown-up neighbors daughters,
And if they was well, 'rainbow,' coveted JOSEPH giggle.

*And lots converted the barrels of moonshine and ignored **Little Joes*** *
as drinks*
there were not FREE.

   *Never mind Little Joe was amongst this lot and knew once the
moon came up and they howled, did be at Little Joe's back door,*
                              THE BORDELLO.
   ***And covertness was rife so ten plagues was about to descend
upon Colville City***

CHAPTER 2 BOOK 2

Johnny Christy and those lethal cigars

"Ha I am alive, and looking about me, free to do what I want, kill two lawmen, maybe just one, the shrimp, the other I will take back to my D.I.Y. A Lincoln self-assembly log cabin, which I will soon move to another warmer spot in Alaska, the south, where big cities are, and LOST BOYS, and not those vampires as I saw the film, 'Lost boys in Alaska visiting from L.A.'

"And why was he so confident, look, wonder, want and go crazy, Colville City folk where settling their covertness' amongst themselves.

Where was the 'asking for help when falling,' well, it was

the 5th July so was still the 4th, and all that mountaineering had made folks thirsty.

And a banjo strummed barn dance music.
Thirty children learning to play the violin joined in.
So did the thirty mothers who already knew how to play a violin.
Then the Colville Barber Quartet, the Fire Department Brass Band, The Temperance Movement Mobile piano on castors and choir, the remains of the Church Choir that had not immigrated beating their pastor, the cats meowing and dogs howling.
It was a din.

And in the newspaper office Father Cindy Lou came out with these words, "I am rich, sold the alien story, "but Mother Cindy Lou being a wife and mother had read his greedy thoughts, "I will take that thank you," and bent down and kissed his head, then with terrific force thrust his wheelchair away.

"My lost wheelchair," the original owner by some miracle walking by emptied Father Cindy Lou out, but not to worry the moonshine turned into **BLOOD.**

"A lynching at last," Mother Cindy Lou stuffing green dollar bills into her brasserie to look bigger and sexier, but she had a mole with hairs growing from it at the end of her chin.

It did not matter how big she got her melons to, those whiskers needed cutting, but she was a lady of tenants, and one was no tattoos or cosmetic surgery, as was a SIN.

So, the ugly mole with the four-inch hairs sprouting from it stayed.

But moonshine and a necktie men thought the sprouting

mole hair sexy, because they was drunk, and the man standing on the back of a cow was Little Joe with a lasso about his neck, and the other end attached to the town barber pole sticking out of a shop building wooden front.

His crime, he had turned **the moonshine into BLOOD.**
The coffee was BLOOD.
Wendy Lou's bath water was BLOOD.

The Big Foot went crazy and pulled planks off house fronts.

Even the bordello and a divorce lawyer did grow rich **as secrets** were revealed at last.

And then the frogs came, and being American frogs were bigger than normal.
"Croak," they croaked a million times so folks ran about looking to stuff soft stuff into the ears.

And there was a lot of soft stuff as Big Foot had visited, and thankfully gone, but came back as liked a frog as a snack.
The town was cursed.

"Almost at the jailhouse," **the strange man** minding his step as them **frogs** wrapped a mile long tongue about you if you stood on one, just before they went 'BANG' and covered you in amphibian gore.

"Buzz," went the **mosquitoes** and **flies** that descended upon the gobbler burgers lying about waiting for mayo and a drunk to gobble.

But the **lice** was silent, they just were there, on all the body hairy parts.

"Ha I am bald," **the strange man** forgetting the other hairy unmentionable anatomical bits, so scratched away and that was a tricky thing to do with missing fingers.

"Where is the pastor, it is his fault for not praying, let us find him," the mob and left Little Joe balancing atop that mule.
"Oh, please do not move cow, a juicy carrot in it."

But the cow had been eating moldy burger buns so was ill, both ends and looked for a field of 4 leaf clover to eat and be healed.
"Oh Gawd, I am stretching," Little Joe stretching.

And the strange man made the jailhouse and entered.

He just stood there knowing the game was up.

Cindy Lou sat there wrapped in a blanket eating chocolate and peanut bars.
So far ten, she was hungry.

The strange man strode forward intent on using his muscle and straggling them all, *'but he was dreaming, how do you strangle folk with a few fingers, I ask you, the fool?'*
And his bare toeless feet stuck to sticky candy bar wrappers, a most uncomfortable feeling.

Then Clay pulled his Colt and fired six times.
Smoke filled the room.

"I thought you was a pacifist Clay?"

And still was because at that point blank range the strange man should be dead, not standing amazed he was not dead.
He snarled.

"Poor Clay was still a pacifist as his automatic nervous system

had fired the Colt in other directions.

And a cat fell onto Little Joes bar top, the stuffed one so do not fret, no live cat was shot."

"Oh no, my tummy been shot again, where is the doctor and which one of them drunks is the doctor?" The pastor who bless him had been praying and do not fret, his bible took the bullet so he could keep praying.

And **ulcers** appeared all over the strange man but not the lawmen as they were heroes and Cindy Lou who had charmed heaven with melody's.

And the big man fell scratching his thousand ulcers.

"Sweep him up deputy," Bottom and Clay dragged the itching man by a leg into a cell and locked himself in with the strange man.
"What have I done Nathan?"

"Kill you," Clay heard and felt hands momentarily on the back of his neck, but the hands were needed for scratching so Clay escaped.

Then the **fiery hailstorm** started breaking the barber pole so Little Joe ran back to his bordello where he was warm, safe, and cozy being read fairy tales with happy endings by his girls.

Then the **locusts** came attracted by the smell of moonshine and flew in the cell window and covered the strange man because he was a bad man.

But a halo hovered over the three others in the goal.
Then "Hey that alien ship is back, quick everyone," and there did seem to be a giant alien spaceship blocking out the sun so all was darkness.

And the strange man made his escape.

He took a deep breath and pulled the jail bras down on the third 'puff.'

"I will take him," and cigar smoke filled the jail, it was choking and a red-hot cigar butt twirled towards the strange man, setting his inflammable trousers alight, then it spread to that spray that he used as a wind breaker and rain stopper, and as he beat the fire out he beat himself out.

Johnny Cash used the jail fire extinguisher on the strange man, the foam then the empty tank, which worked a treat.

Then two men in black with sunglasses appeared, from where, **it is a secret.**

"We will take him, The Mounties want him," Johnny and played mouth organ music.

"And the 'WE,' was 'MEN in BLACK,' "and being curious wondered if they were all in black and peeked, nope, one was in white shorts with a TIGRE face printed on front, whose he kidding, and the other was just a yellow willy warmer, on the small size, THEN:

"HAVE YOU LEARNED NOTHING?" And felt energy whack the back of my head, that felt it.

"Yeh, to love Joseph as my neighbor and still be me, A HARLOT."

Boss Angel hugged me, not for my cheek but for letting him sneak Fili Pek into the hug.

"Love thy neighbor," Boss Angel and did not grunt, he was learning from me.

After grimacing, *"Come here Fili Pek,"* and felt him hate me, loath me, want to destroy me as we both knew what I meant, I could have called him 'Joseph.'

Unfortunately, Boss angel felt and read his energy so; *"No, forgive Fili Pek,"* as Joseph was tossed down a portal to vacate a while in THE OUTER DARKNESS and be cure dof his hate for little me.

I finished rolling down my stockings, I would always be Boss Angels' favorite, a woman just knows how to win, snort, giggle.

"S**T," Number Two behind the scenes.

Anyway, The Men in Black put the strange man into BALL AND CHAINS as he was going to the chain gang and sing a different type of melodious tune, "WE are working on the chain gang, here comes the train."

Where did the heavy Ball and Chains appear from, they took them from their deep pockets **so is not a secret.**
And Johnny Christy used the uncovered mouth of the strange man as an ashtray.

Smoke and flames appeared, but it was just the strange man so what?

"F*** you bas*****," he did manage to cough between the puffs of smoke.

Then Clay restored my faith in humanity and New Age Music, he pored a cup of stale coffee with a top of green mold down the strange man's throat and put out the fires of hell within.

"Thank you, you will always be my Clay Eagle Pin Up when I serve my 'Jailhouse Rock' time."

I never seen Clay Eagle get arrested for murder but he came close as he grabbed the slop bucket mop and washed out the strange man's mouth.

"Leave him to us Clay," Johnny and The Men in Black, well they levitated the strange man out into the back of 'A TEAM TRANSIT VAN.'

At the driver's window an American Black Man with a green Mohican revving the V12 engine.
Loud exciting music belched from the exhaust.

By the way, the van was electric and the revving and exhaust illusionary effects.
Father Cindy Lou fell out the back, was picked up and thrown in again.

"Do not forget Mother Cindy Lou," Sheriff Bottom hopefully.

"Why she sold to the newspapers about an alien flying saucer and little green Martians shopping in Colville City also?" The Men in Black in unison.

Then with mouth organ music coming from the passenger window, remember the A TEAM TRANSIT was wide, because that Afro American had a big seat, then all, the other heroes crammed in also, the thirty of them, and for the Lord of it cannot remember their names.
"Raw Hide,
Round them,
Brand them,
Eat them," Johnny sang obviously disgusted with gobbler burgers and wanting the real Mckay.

And the town looked spotless, those Big Foot critters not

wanting publicity had swept, picked up, gobbled up, put away, litter.

And as the A TEAM TRANSIT VAN drove down Main Street, Johnny Christy took imaginary pot shots at the ten giant citizens in top hats and coats, the five ugly Nannies pushing the ugliest babies ever, and the two fury pastors with dog collars that seemed to be choking the wearers.

He knew who they really were, but just like were they were going, Area 51, **it was a secret.**
Big Foot was safe.

*

"Johnny you been promoted to special agent first class, five star, and America is grateful to you," it looked like President Truman, but was a mask, and behind that presidential mask, an important person, a male, a girl, army, navy, air force, politician, **was a secret.**

And Johnny stuffed the one hundred thousand dollars into his sombrero zip pouches and played his mouth organ as he walked away, home,

"To where the antelope roam,
 Raw Hide,
 Round them,
 Brand them,
 Sell them," and he vanished, was that him roaring away in a huge mobile holiday home, heading north, but where, **a secret.**

*

"Think I will give my laundry to Wendy Lou," Clay eyeing his boss, Nathan who eyed him back and they was both eyed by Cindy Lou.

And slowly the two men inches then trotted and sprinted to the front door of Wendy Lou's, followed by Cindy Lou.

"Where the hell did that come from?" Sheriff Bottom ogling the huge holiday mobile home parked illegally outside Wendy's house.

"I smell cigar," Clay and was correct and a cigar butt lit landed atop his deputy hat and set it on fire.

Nathan saw his chance and galloped past and collided with a banjo.

"I got a nosebleed darn hot jalapenos," he swore loudly.

Then the huge mobile home drove away choking them in dust.

"Bye boys," the boys were sure they heard Wendy Lou call from the passenger window of that huge mobile home.

"Well at least we have Cindy Lou as compensation," Clay picking his words wisely.

"Yeh, she can hold a kerchief to my bloody nose then cook my dinner," Sheriff Bottom showing wisdom in his phraseology.

"Bu**** off," Cindy Lou and ran after the mobile home that had stopped to wait for her.

How did Johnny know she did want to join the expedition to sunny California, all expenses paid?
It is a secret.

"Bye," Sheriff Bottom waving a small hand at the back of the disappearing huge mobile home.

"Meana, Meana," Clay knowing there did always be a

tomorrow, and is what happened today that is important.

It was FRIDAT night of course and Colville City came alive.

And hundreds of loggers, gold panners, monster hunters, paranormal investigators, alien photographers, and tourists, plus the monsters later
to clean up,
guzzle up,
run down and up,
MAIN STREET.

"Look at it this way Clay, we still got Little Joes," as they watched him and his girls use new planking to shore up the bordello.

"Yeh we still got Granny Cindy Lou, I think I am needed in Fairbanks," Clay making a getaway to his patrol car.

"Hello sweetie," Granny Cindy Lou, and she was responsible for the ex-friends becoming friends again as Sheriff Bottom jumped through the closed side window, and why Clay had to stop the car and drag his friend in, then drive away.

A hundred yards down the road the laughter of a maniacal witch came from the back of that patrol car. Never the less it caused the patrol car to run off the road into the Coville River.

How did Granny Cindy Lou get in that patrol car unnoticed?
A secret.

And the patrol car floated down to Fairbanks where the boys did spend the reward money on themselves and an Amazon Prime Delivery Special Same Day Delivery; Granny was sent back to Colville, and as the lawmen were not meanies, let her borrow the 'delivero man.'

"Thank Tonka we got rid of her," Clay being fed grapes by floozy hostesses in a Casino swimming pool.

"Thank Sweet Jesus she is gone," Sheriff Bottom allowing a floozy hostess to polish his ten-gallon hat.

And "Tee, he, I am so happy I got all this reward money I found in the back pockets of those hero boys, wonder how they are going to pay the bills they are running up," a wicked Granny Cindy Lou.

And that part is definitely a secret.

THE END.

ACKNOWLEDGEMENT

Thank you Alaska for this crazy ridiculous fun tale
or would not be written.
Thank you Big Foot.

ABOUT THE AUTHOR

Keith Hulse

Keith was an archaeologist, soldier, entrepreneur, Scottish War Blinded Veteran.
Stories come tumbling into my left temple and out the right ear.
Spirit people visit him, his house is full of cats, perhaps why.

BOOKS BY THIS AUTHOR

Tiberius Grant:non Illustrated

The Way
Starts of as a trial
Transmigration of the soul
Ancient Celtic lore
The way is way of life
Anti-war
Love story
Tiberius the Ram
His loves
Evil of big business and owners, Presidents and
Corrupt rulers.
Is for the protection of life, eco system, planets
to come our way.
About the way
Celtic and Mexican way

Tiberius Grant, Illustrated Version

The Way
Starts of as a trial
Transmigration of the soul
Ancient Celtic lore
The way is way of life

ILLUSTRATED
The Way

Starts of as a trial
Transmigration of the soul
Ancient Celtic lore
The way is way of life
Anti-war
Love story
Tiberius the Ram
His loves
Evil of big business and owners, Presidents and
Corrupt rulers.
Is for the protection of life, eco system, planets
to come our way.
About the way
Celtic and Mexican way

Mingo Drum Vercingetorix, Illustrated

Mingo Drum Vercingetorix, Birdman, King of the Artebrates,
Fighting aliens, Human and amphibian Madrawt, for his home,
Planet Maponos.
Based on the history of ancient Gaul, and Native American
Indian Tribes, when they met
A superior military machine.
No longer single heroic warrior combat.
This loved story is a tearjerker but twists into a happy ending.

Ants 169 Non Illustrated

This is the non-illustrated version of Ants 169 illustrations,
Books One and Two together.
It is designed for paperback and library submission.
True to the original story, Luke rides a giant Black Ant, Utna in
his war against
humanoid insects.
Genetically altered from radiation fallout and gene shuttling.

Adventure and romance with Luke as he fights for humankind.
From boyhood into a man, the pains of growing, physically and spiritually.
Row the Insect war galleys with Luke as a rower.
Swim with Luke away from sharks in the Yellow Sea as his galley sinks.
A good read.
Concluding happy ending for all books.

Ants 169 [Revised Illustrations] Science Fiction

Queen Nina sees winged insects as base.
Luke, a man who rides a giant ant, change places with him by using imagination.
He races across the grass, wind on him, afraid of nothing for Utna his ant is big.
Could be you, imagine.
Visit see the fauna.
Take your camera for strange beasts exist.
World has another secret, humans who are not slaves. And the Insect God Enil with no wings has a secret too.

Mungo, Books One And Two.

97334 words, 450 pages, illustrated.
A mammoth adventure for Mungo, the boy raised by lions on New Uranus, humanoid, all creatures here are about humanoid thanks to genetic engineering.
Of his first love, Sasha, daughter of Red Hide, King of Lions, to his war with Carman, Queen of Lizard Folk.
These lizard folk like humans at a barbecue, as the burgers, steaks, and sausages.
No wonder Mungo wars against them.
And no one wins in a war as a human star ship arrives and enslaves the lot.
Advanced humans see other humans as undesirables.

Run through the red grass, climb giant rhododendron flowers, smell the clean air of the mountains, and only found here with Mungo the lion rider.

Spiritually awakening as Luke when does good beams Light, but when does bad, becomes dark.

A sub book runs in it, 'Mazarrats,' who comically provide sarcastic comment.

Mungo, Book One.

50632 words, 201 pages.

Mungo travels his world to the floating city of Huverra.

Meet his friends and enemies.

Meet more mazarrats as they provide a parallel story.

Mazarrats a cross between a mongoose and a baboon is said.

Not true, they are cute singers looking for a home.

Mazarrats, you want to take home with you.

They run a story themselves between the lines.

Discover the technological wonders these lizard folks have.

Ghost Wife, A Comedy Melee

74256 words, 159 pages, illustrated.

Oh, Morag dear, you died so do what ghosts do, Rest In Peace.

"Not on your Nelly, I am very much alive, and stop ogling the medium Con, dear." Plenty of madcap ridiculous fun. Information on the After Life.

Is comic mayhem, fanciful rubbish to tickle. The ghosts here will not haunt but make you laugh, so do not worry about holding bibles, these ghosts are clowns.

Ghost Romance, A Comedy Of Errors

54980 words, 218 words, illustrated.

A nonstop ghostly ridiculous adventure from Borneo to New York Zoo, with Calamity the orangutan in tow. So, load up on bananas and figs as the ape eats non-stop.

"Ouk," is her only word spoken.

Do not worry about the extras feeding the crocodiles, they come under a dime a dozen and are not in any union, and better, made of indigestible rubber.

Not to worry animal lovers, a vet is on standby by for the sweet crocodiles, sea water variety so bigger, nastier, fierce, and wanting you as food.

This book speaks heaps for food out there, a mixture of local, Indian, Chinese, Portuguese, Dutch, British, you name it, it found a way onto the menu.

Eat more than a banana and drink condensed tea milk to sweeten you up.

Coachman, A Travelers Laughing Melody

159340 words 577 pages

Non-illustrated.

Aggressive comedy

Exciting travel adventure.

Spiritual element all covet the sparkle so all unhappy getting it.

Ah, the sparkle is what the thieving pretty ankle beat out

Of Dwarf, which is his name and proud of it.

And she escapes to get as far away as the coach takes her.

Except the coach picks up passengers, Dwarf for one.

ALL AFTER THE SPARKLE for they covet wealth. Nothing wrong with that, except when it involves nasty Grannies, were-wolfs, cowboy sheriffs, Lancelot and as oily Mr. Oiler salesperson related to the famous Hood Bros.

In this tale escape to a parallel dimension and forget the horrors of ours.

Eagor The Monster, A Laughing Tale: Not Illustrated

About Eagor's dealings with The Hoods, cousins who would sell stuffed grannies in wheelchairs if they could.

Eagor although ugly has girlfriends.

From were-wolf to pretty royalty. Eagor is a two timing monster. Deserves what he gets and gets it from angry bears to jealous women.

We could learn a trick or two from this fake of a monster.

But he does make you laugh as he is a foolish monster needing your sympathy, love,

cuddle, never as Eagor is strong as when he hugs Badbladder, you hear the sound of snapping bones.

Not to worry the witch Morag has lose bits upstairs so spells lose to, wonderful news, all healed just liked that.

All live in Forgotten Land, so visit as a tourist and buy a jar of leeches, that the HOODS swear cure all, your bad breath, breathlessness, itchy skin and lack of iron for starters.

Buy at discount, come be a tourist, visit strong Eagor for a hug and never be the same again..

Same time a spiritual current as 'One must die for many,' taken from scriptures but here no one dies, they just live happily ever after like you can.

Eagor The Monster, A Laughing Tale: Illustrated

AS ABOVE

Printed in Great Britain
by Amazon

84228820R00133